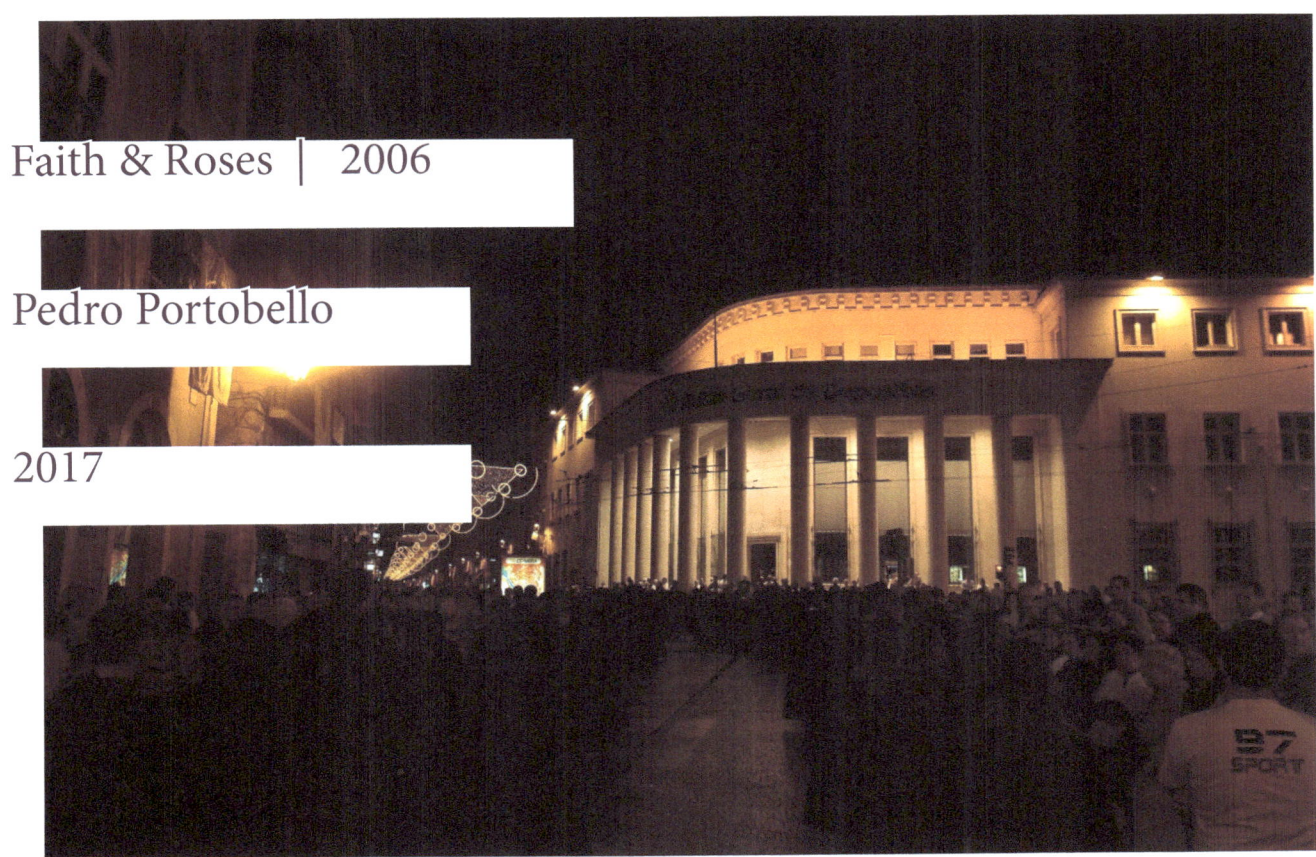

Faith & Roses | 2006

Pedro Portobello

2017

Pedro Portobello was born in Lobito, Angola, in 1958.

He obtained his Ph.D. in Communication Sciences (2005) and degrees in Journalism (1999) and Law (1981) at the University of Coimbra.

He is a Professor at the Instituto Superior Miguel Torga (Coimbra), and led the Degree in Social Communication course until 2017.

He is also a Visiting Professor at the Institute of Information Sciences and Administration (Iscia - Aveiro), a Consultant in Communication for the Port of Aveiro (APA) and the Portuguese Ports Association (APP).

Formerly a journalist for portuguese publications and stations "TSF", "Expresso", "Grande Reportagem", "TVI", "Tal & Qual" and the "Jornal de Coimbra", Dinis still undertakes work as a photo-journalist.

He is also the author of several photography exhibitions and websites, accessible through dmareport.blogspot.pt

As a deputy in the Portuguese Parliament (Socialist Party), Dinis worked in partnership with Jaime Ramos (Social Democrat Party) to sponsor the first project to create local radio stations in Portugal (1983).

He has over two dozen books and photo albums published.

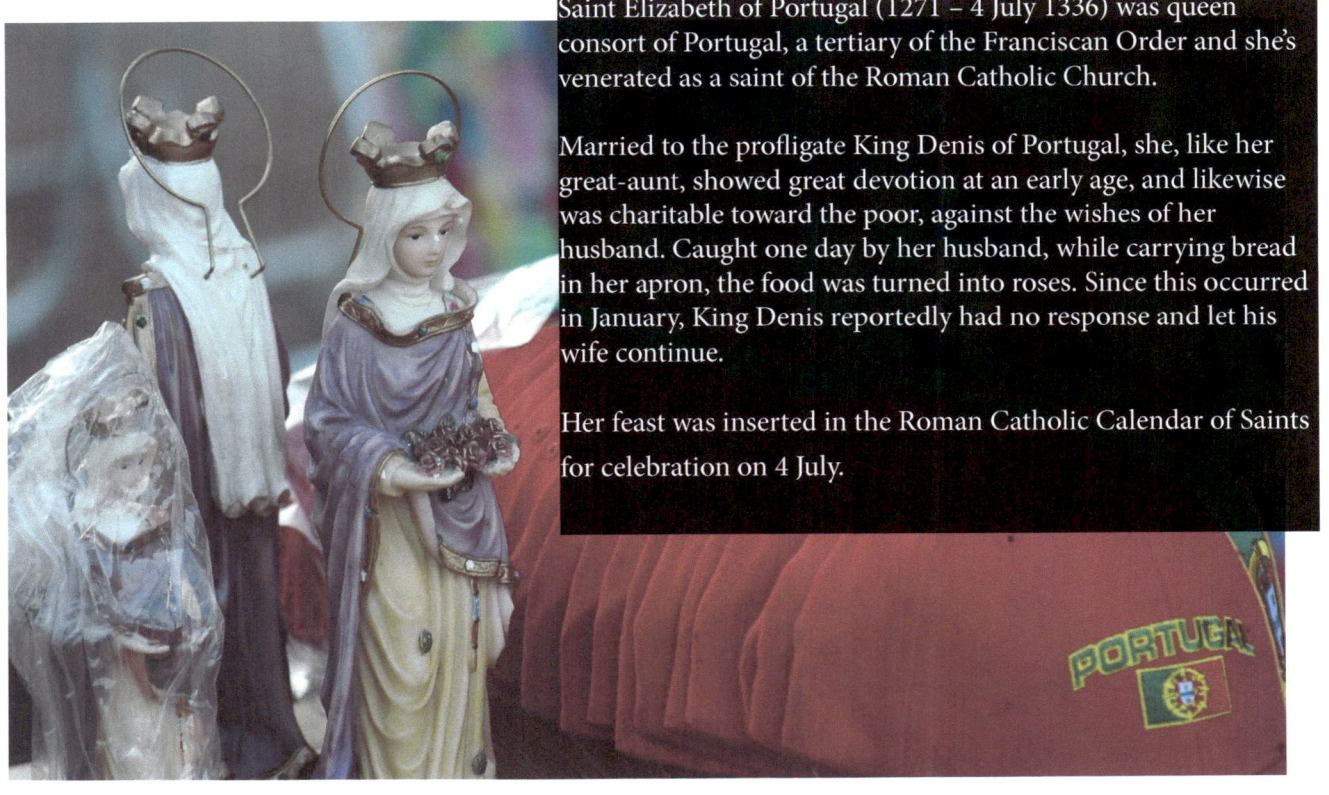

Saint Elizabeth of Portugal (1271 – 4 July 1336) was queen consort of Portugal, a tertiary of the Franciscan Order and she's venerated as a saint of the Roman Catholic Church.

Married to the profligate King Denis of Portugal, she, like her great-aunt, showed great devotion at an early age, and likewise was charitable toward the poor, against the wishes of her husband. Caught one day by her husband, while carrying bread in her apron, the food was turned into roses. Since this occurred in January, King Denis reportedly had no response and let his wife continue.

Her feast was inserted in the Roman Catholic Calendar of Saints for celebration on 4 July.

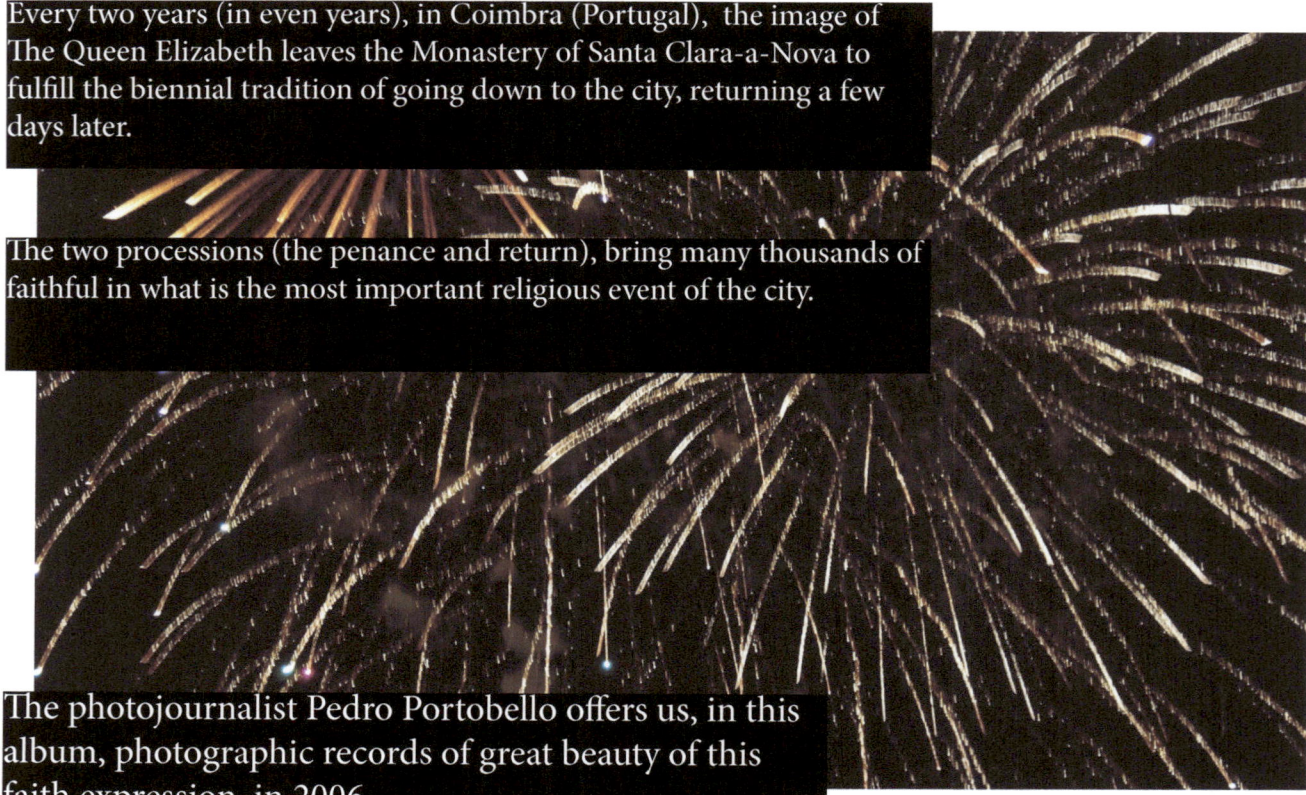

Every two years (in even years), in Coimbra (Portugal), the image of The Queen Elizabeth leaves the Monastery of Santa Clara-a-Nova to fulfill the biennial tradition of going down to the city, returning a few days later.

The two processions (the penance and return), bring many thousands of faithful in what is the most important religious event of the city.

The photojournalist Pedro Portobello offers us, in this album, photographic records of great beauty of this faith expression, in 2006.

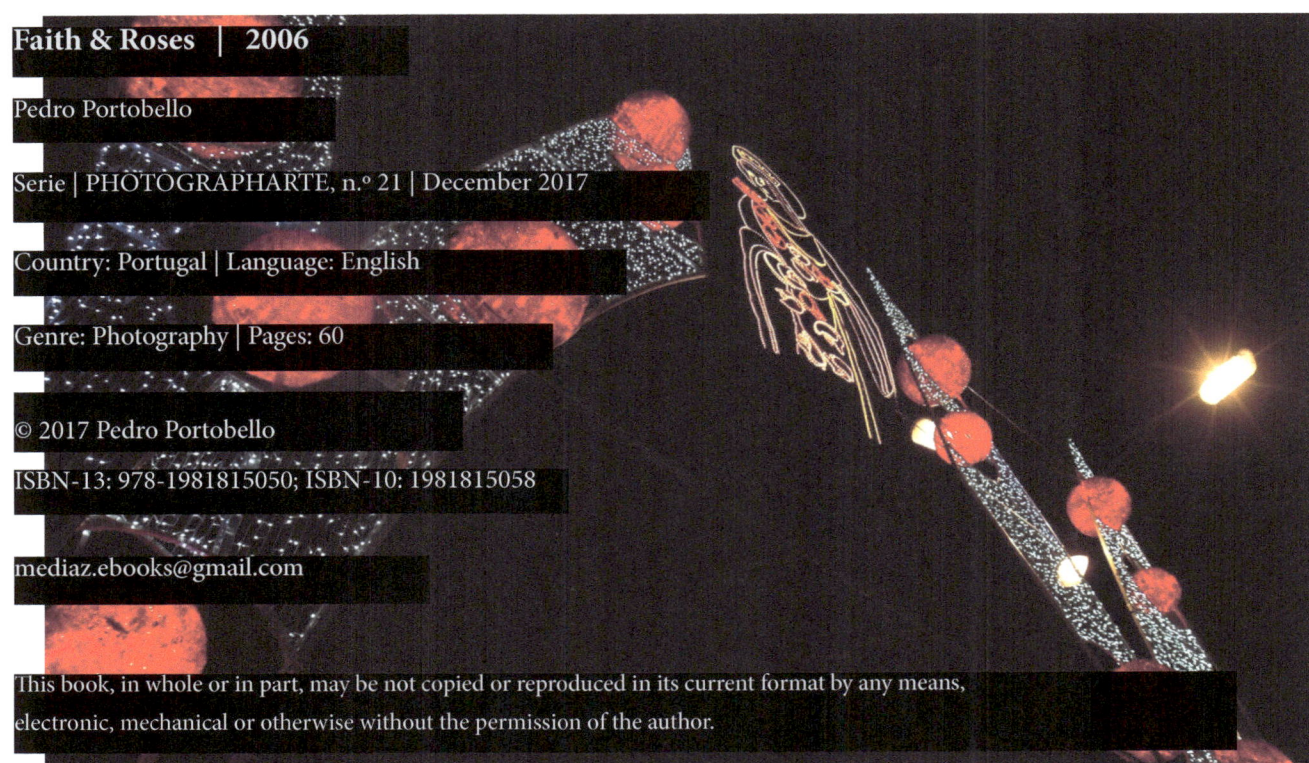

Faith & Roses | 2006

Pedro Portobello

Serie | PHOTOGRAPHARTE, n.º 21 | December 2017

Country: Portugal | Language: English

Genre: Photography | Pages: 60

© 2017 Pedro Portobello

ISBN-13: 978-1981815050; ISBN-10: 1981815058

mediaz.ebooks@gmail.com

This book, in whole or in part, may be not copied or reproduced in its current format by any means, electronic, mechanical or otherwise without the permission of the author.

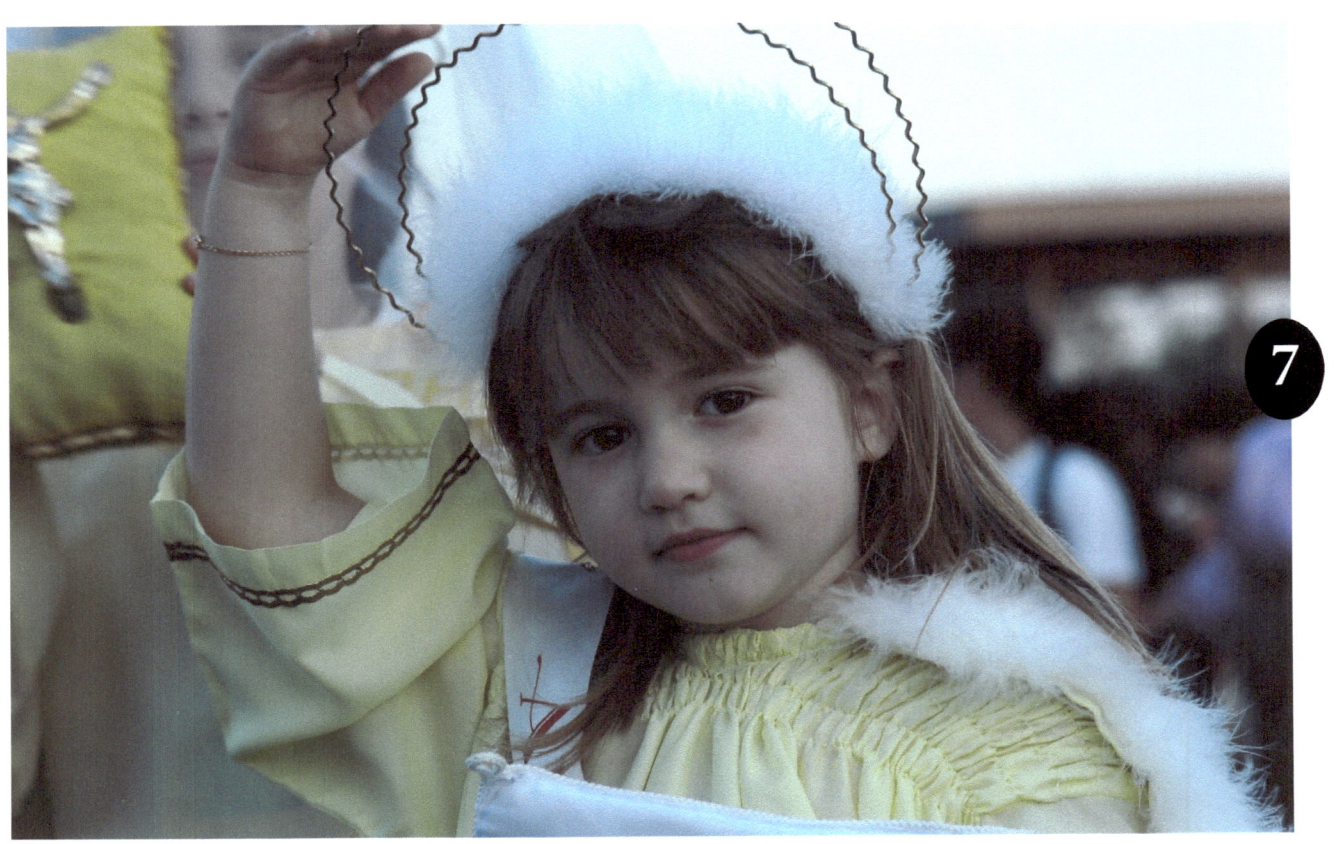

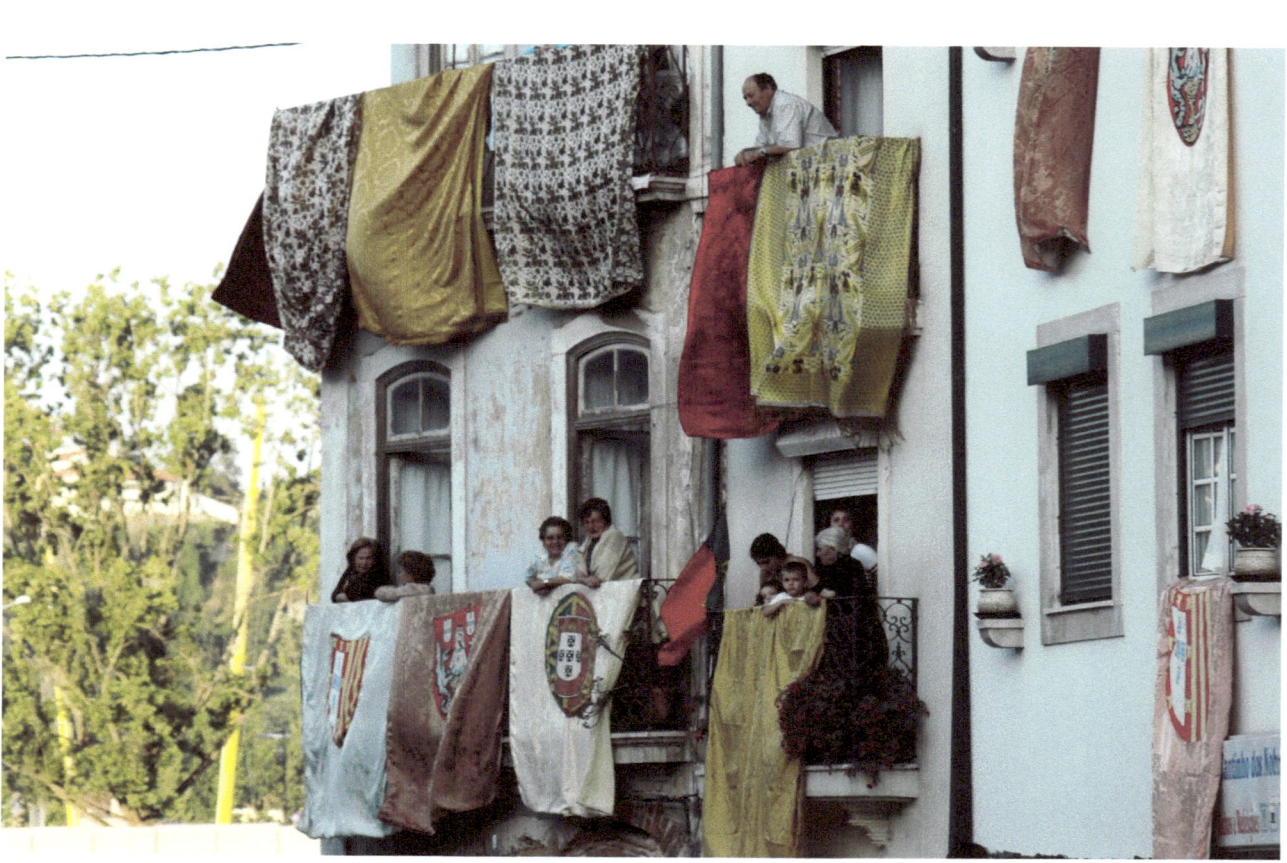

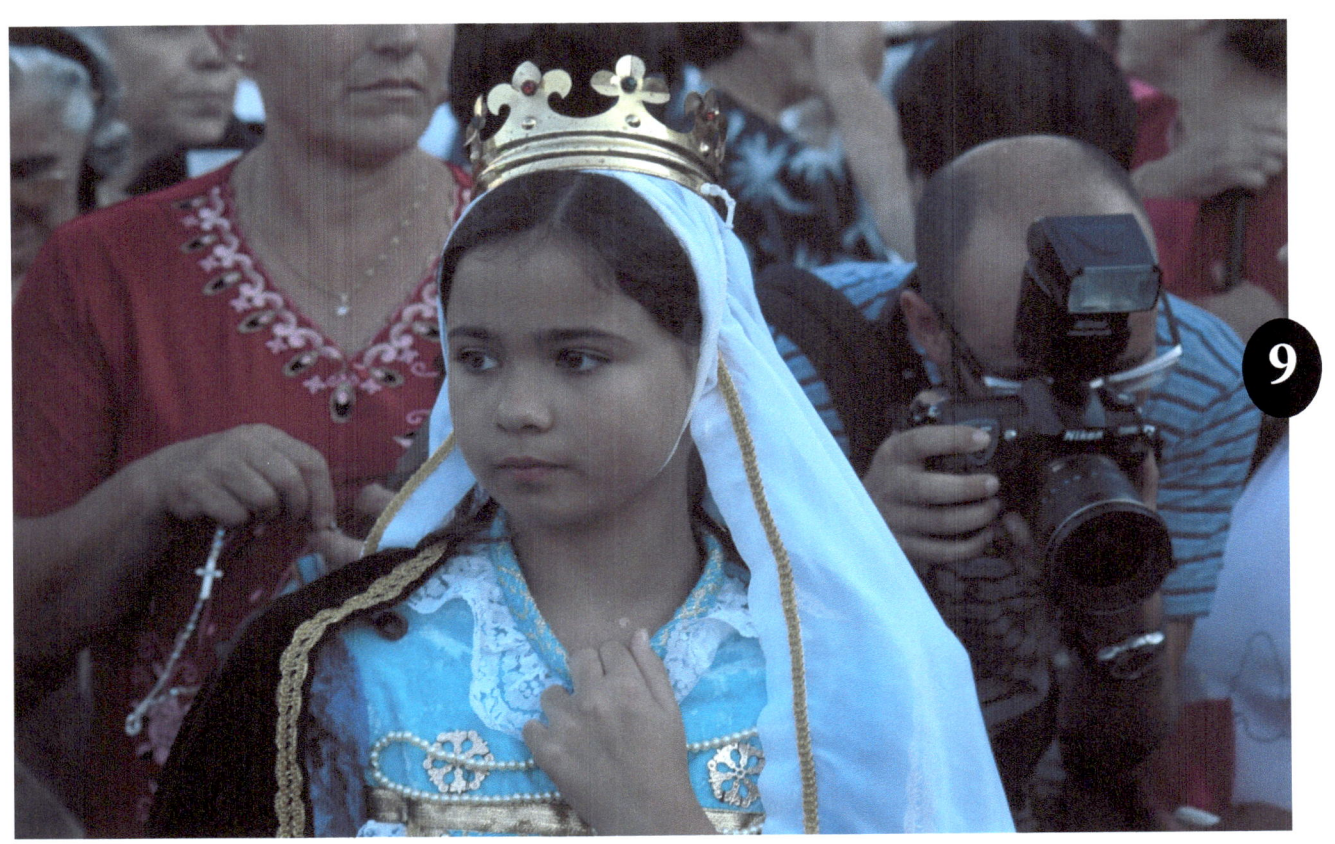

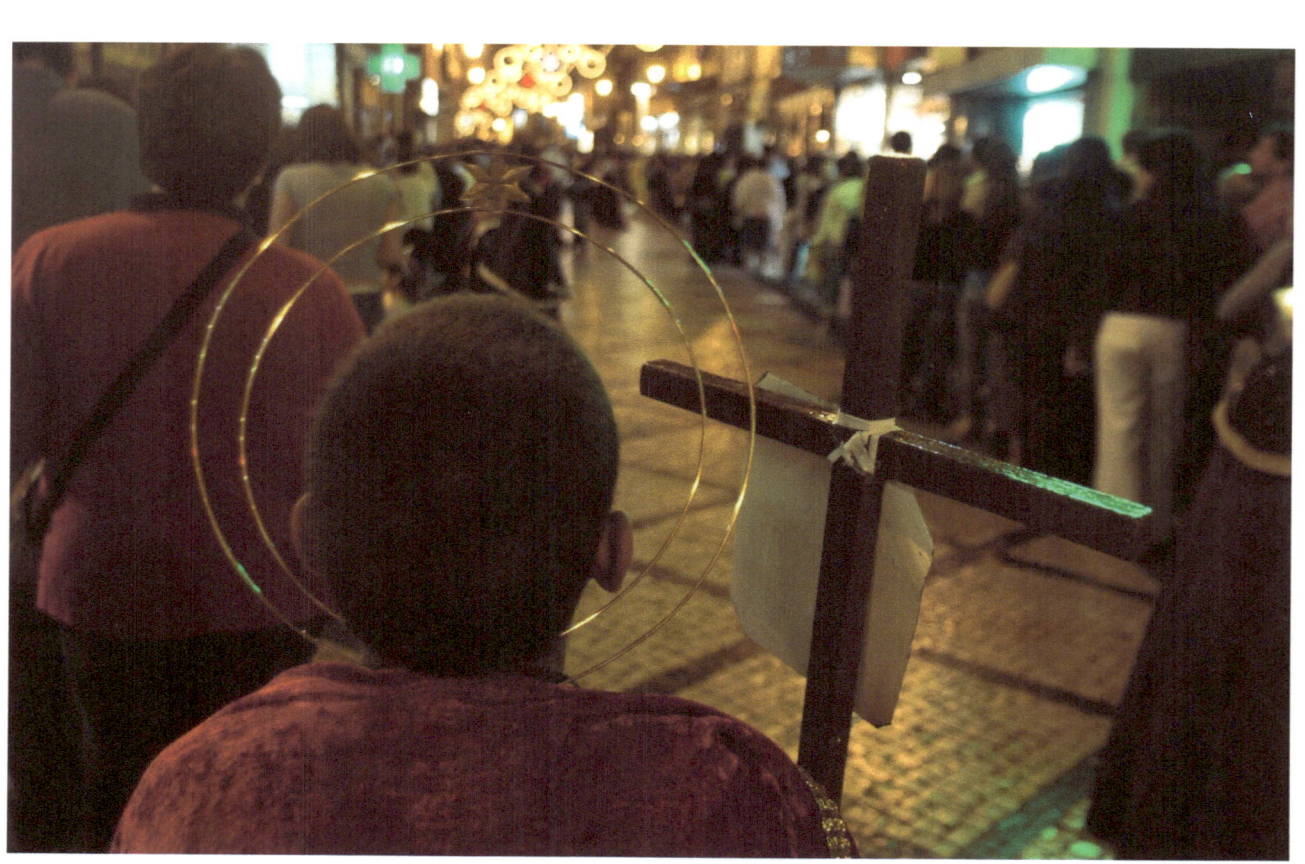

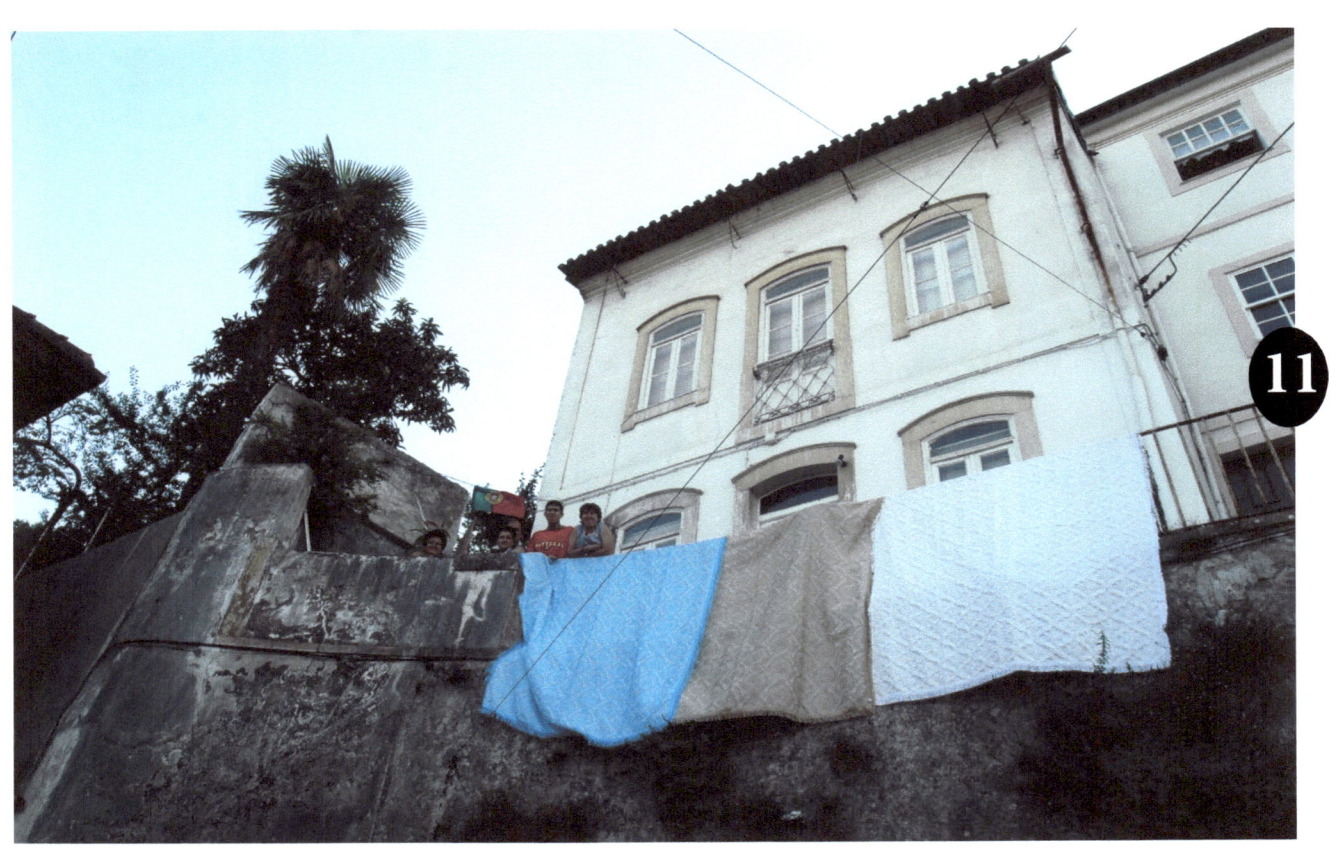

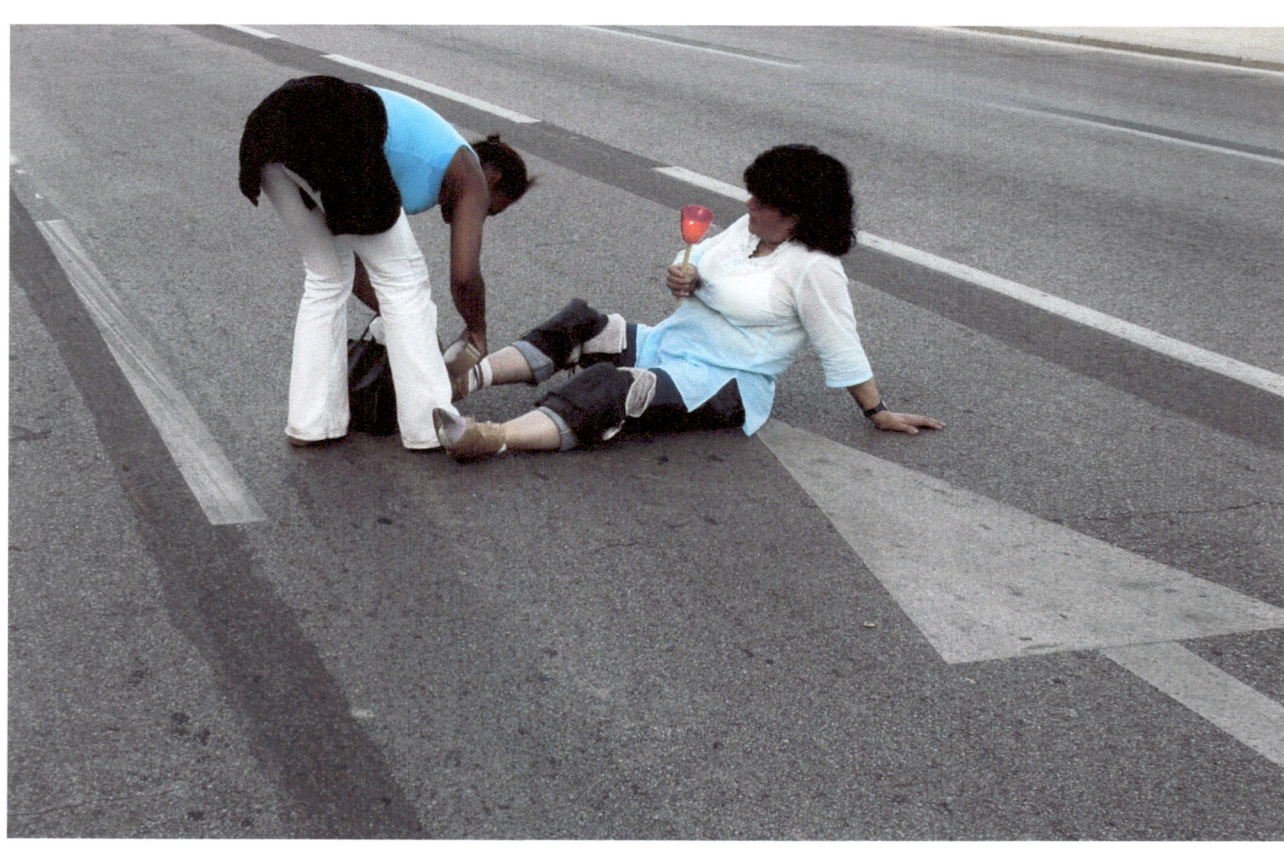

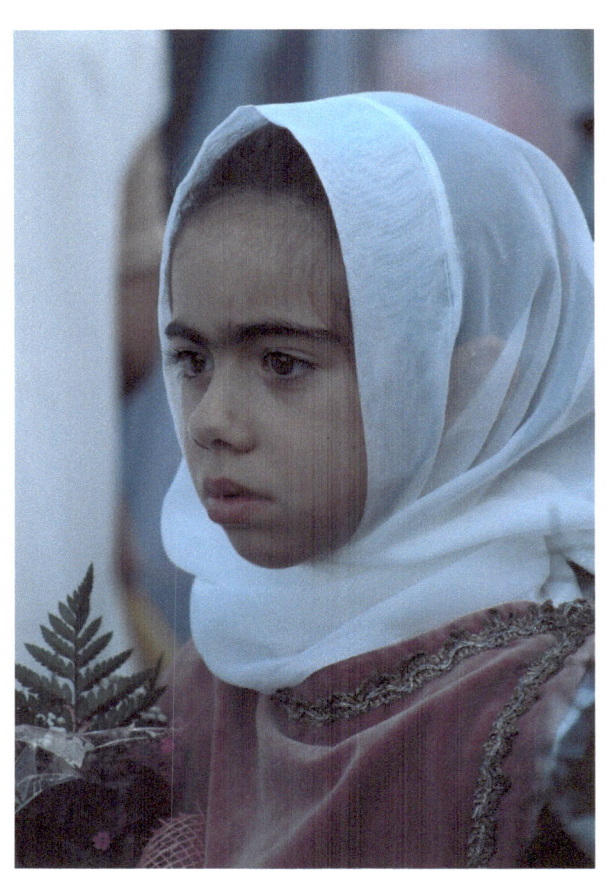
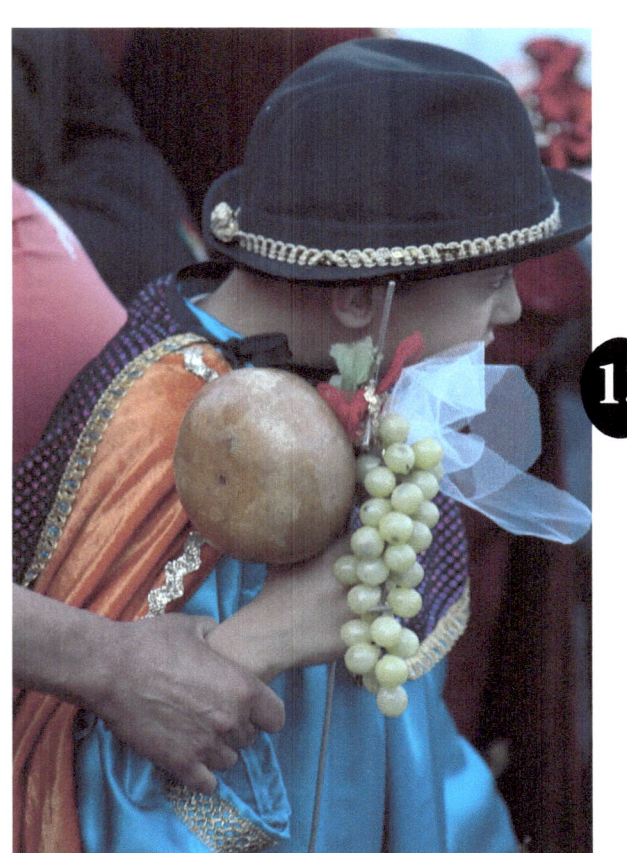

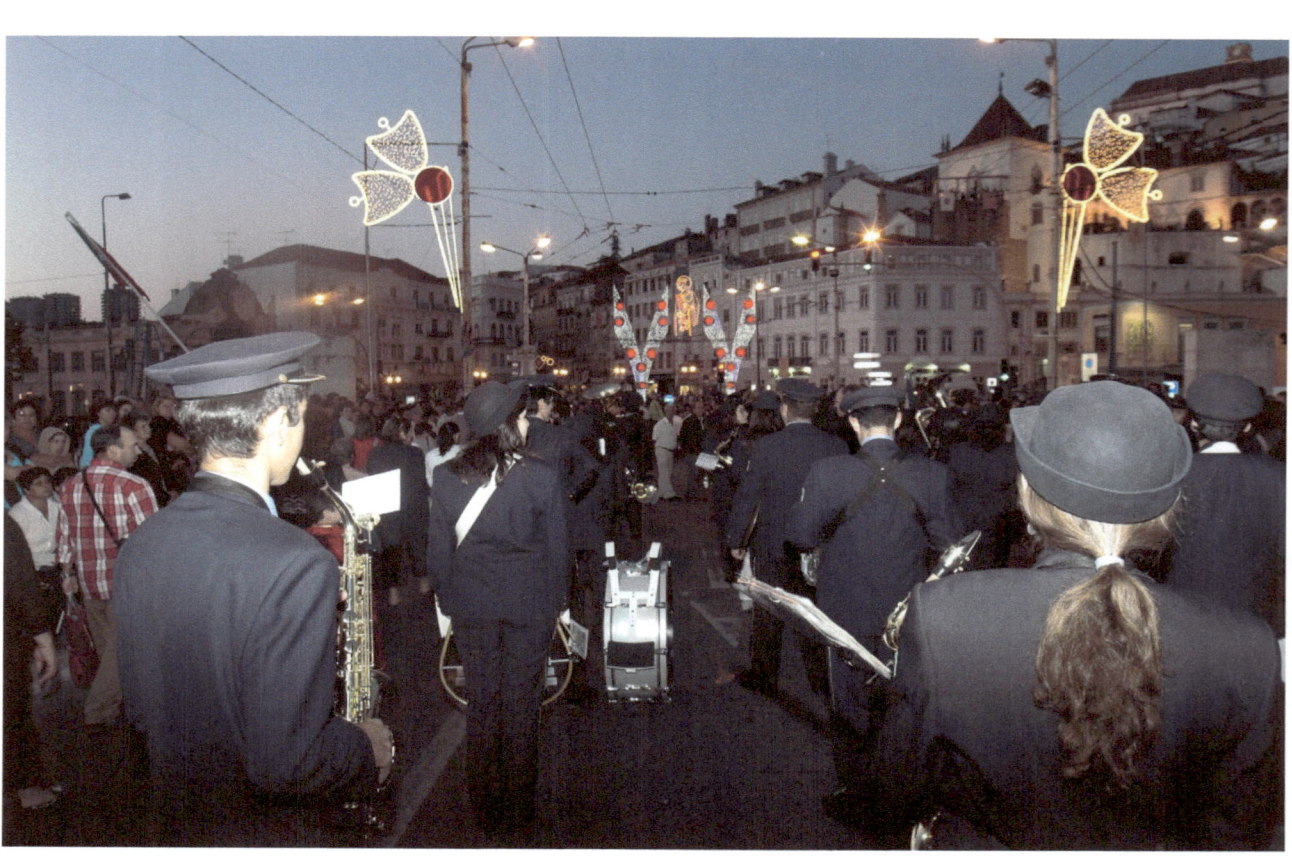

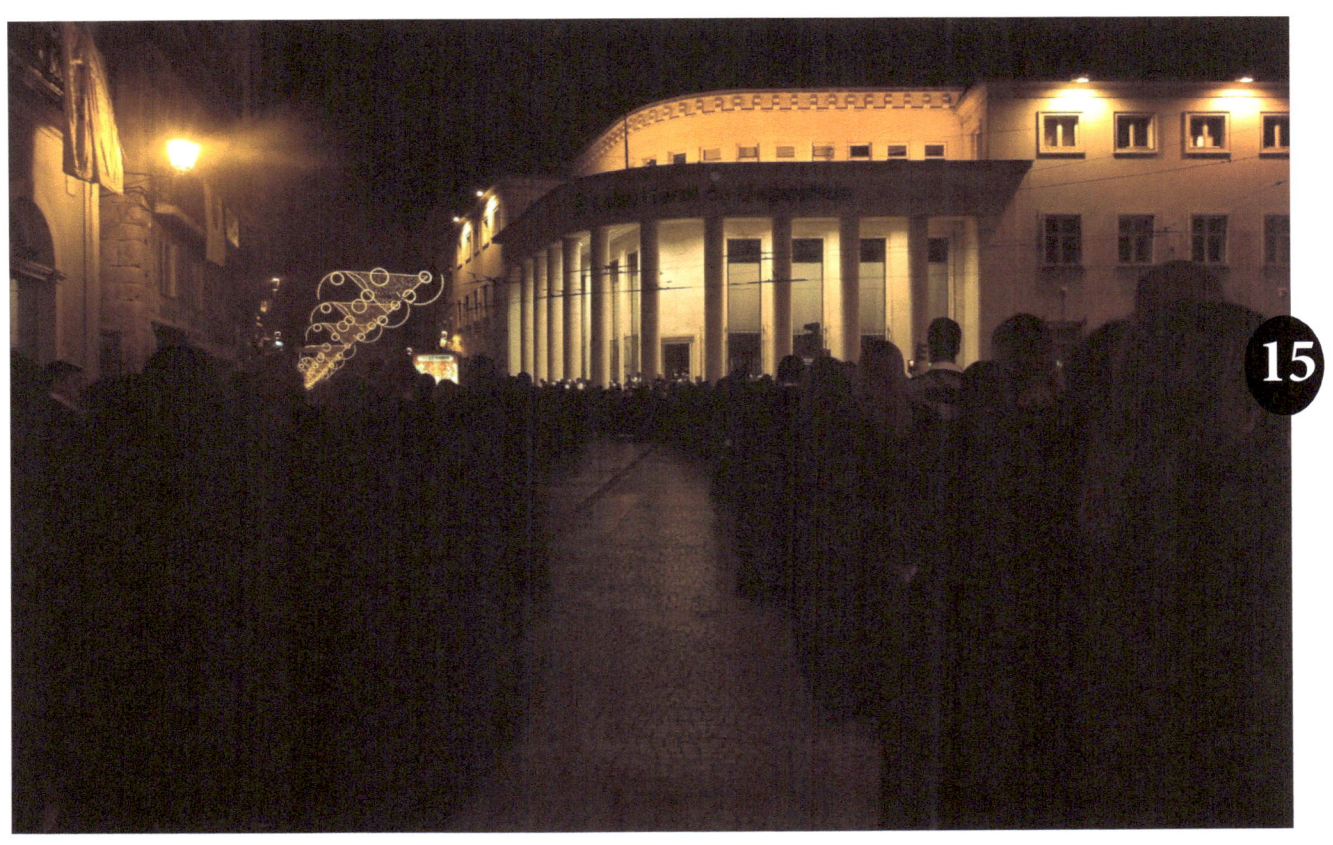

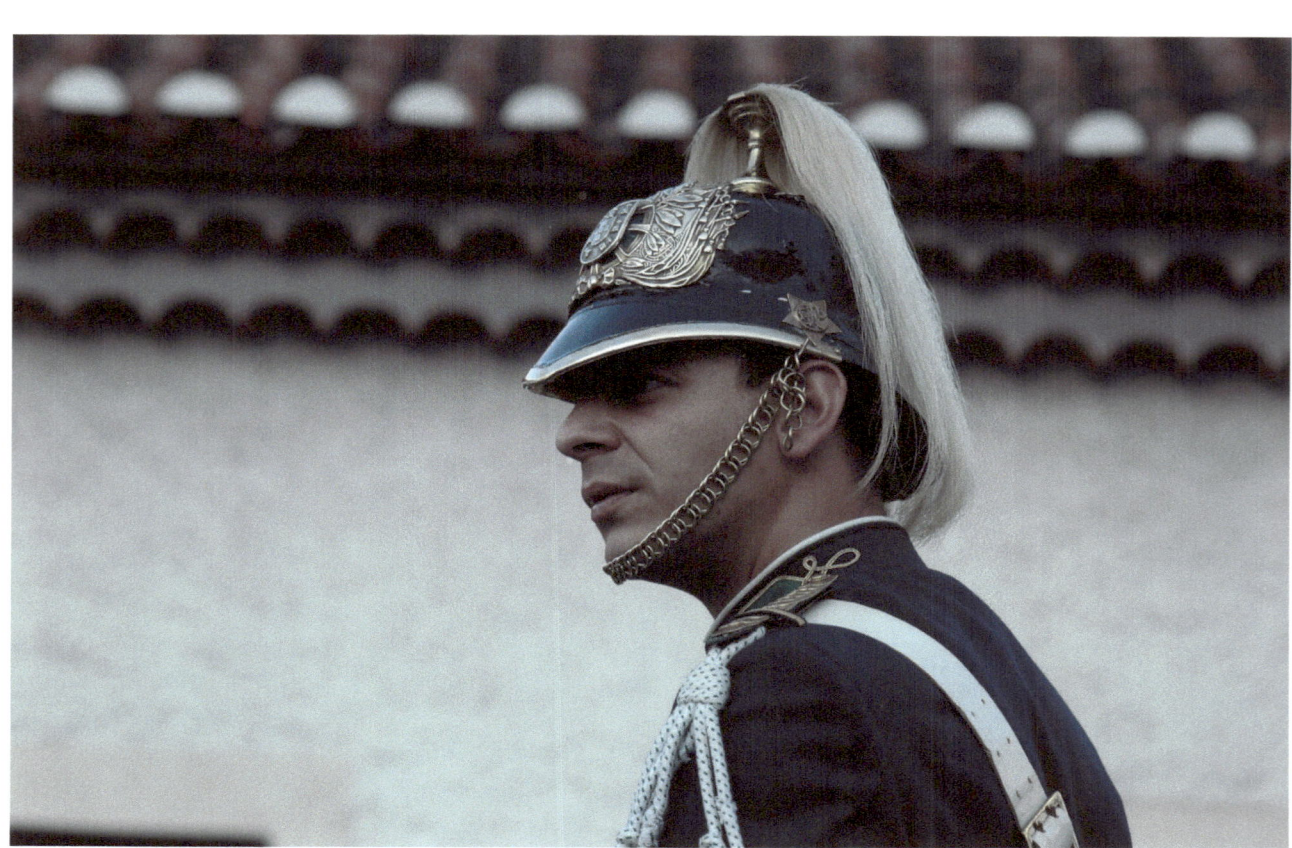

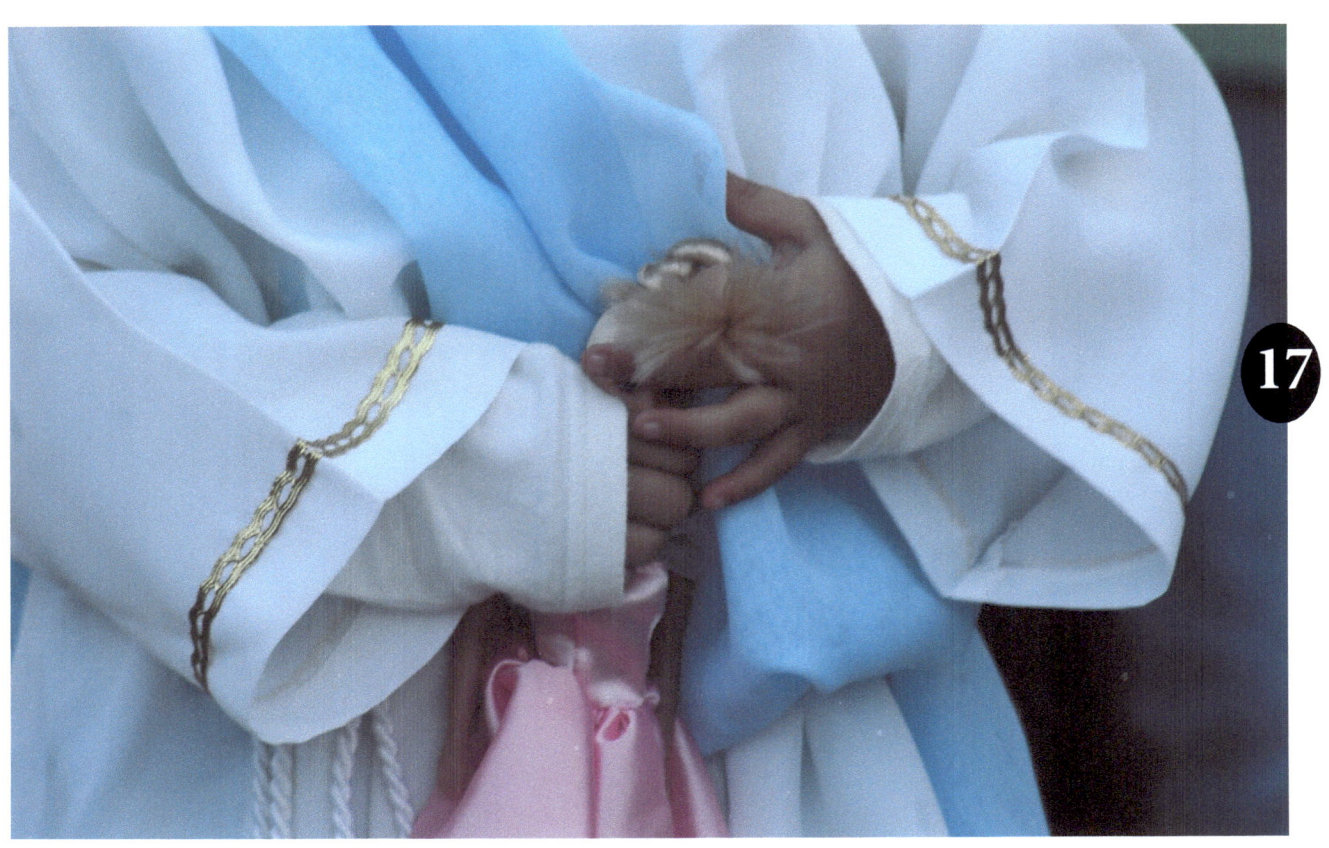

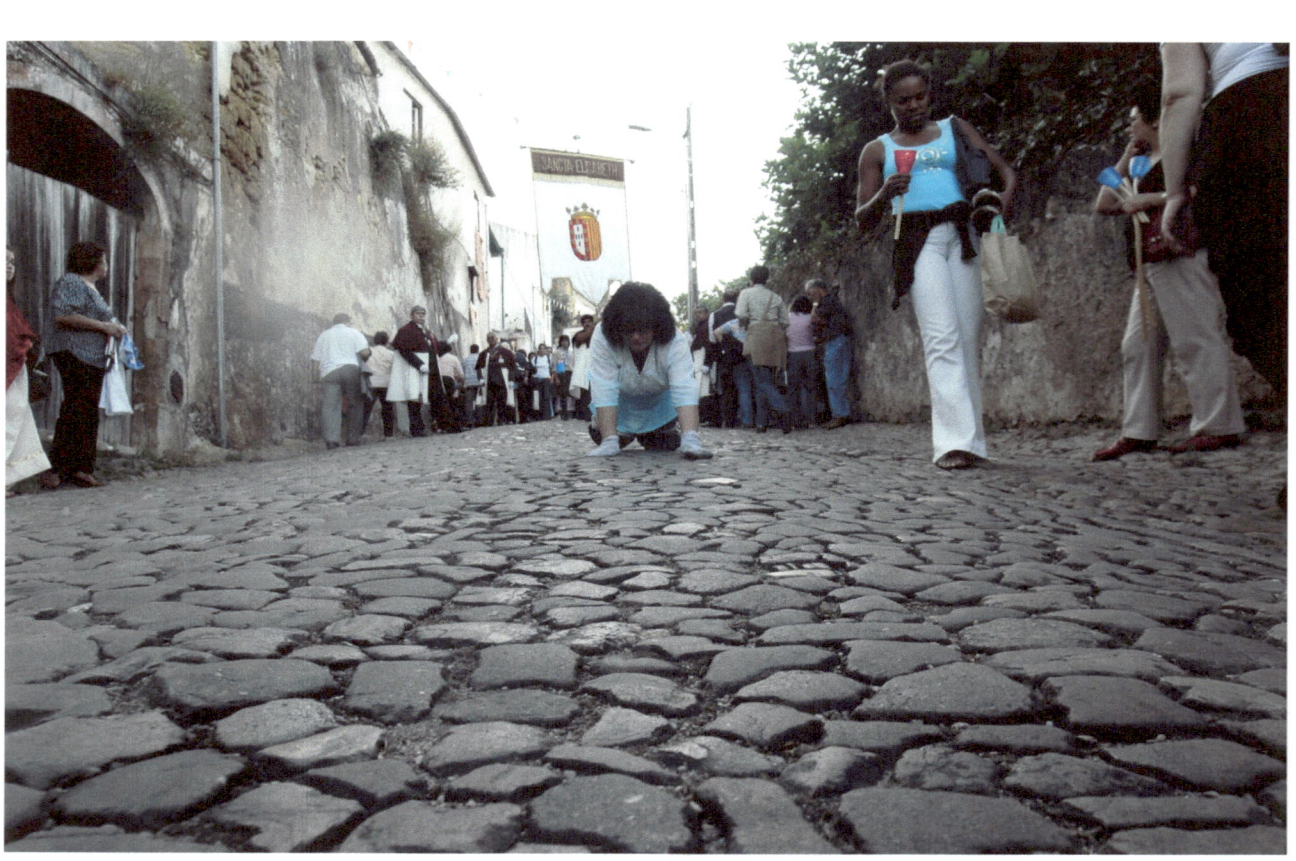

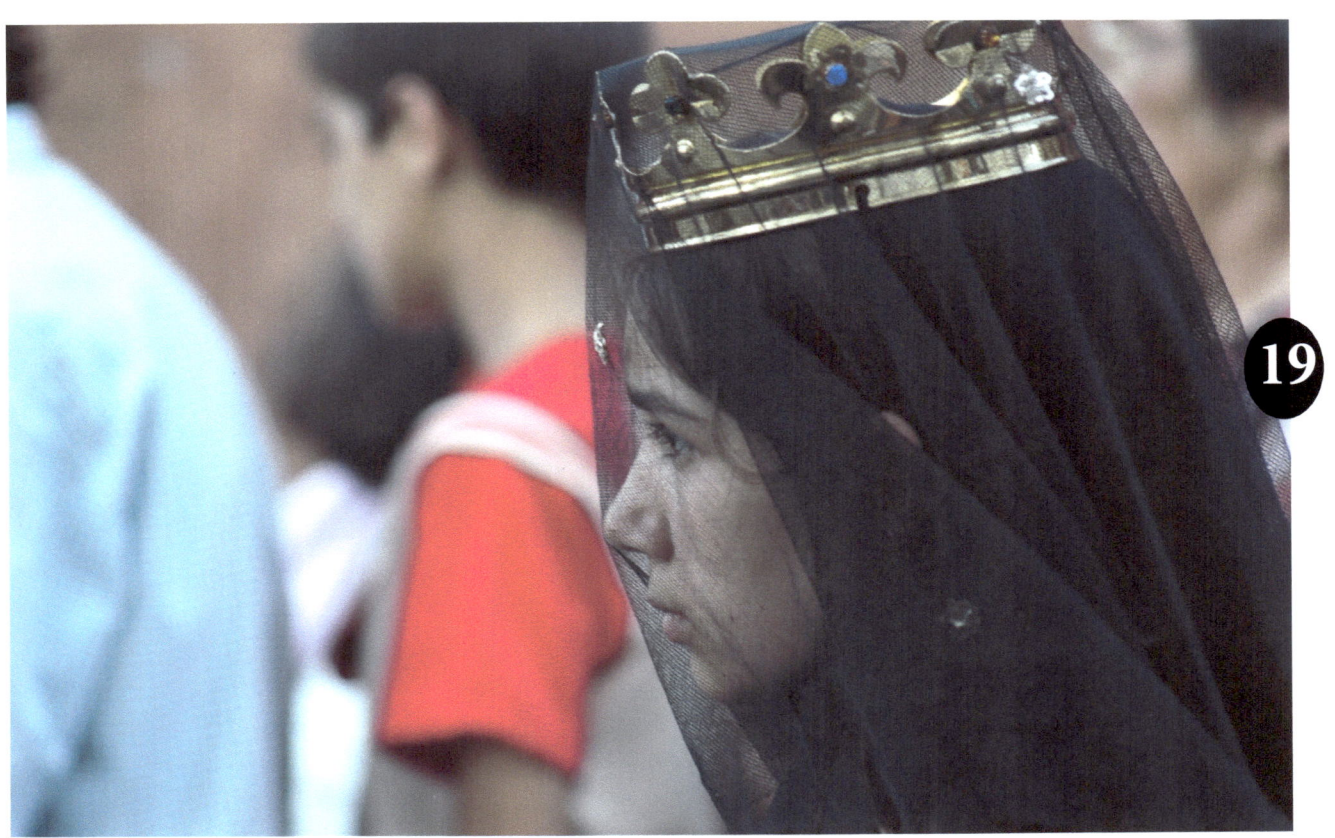

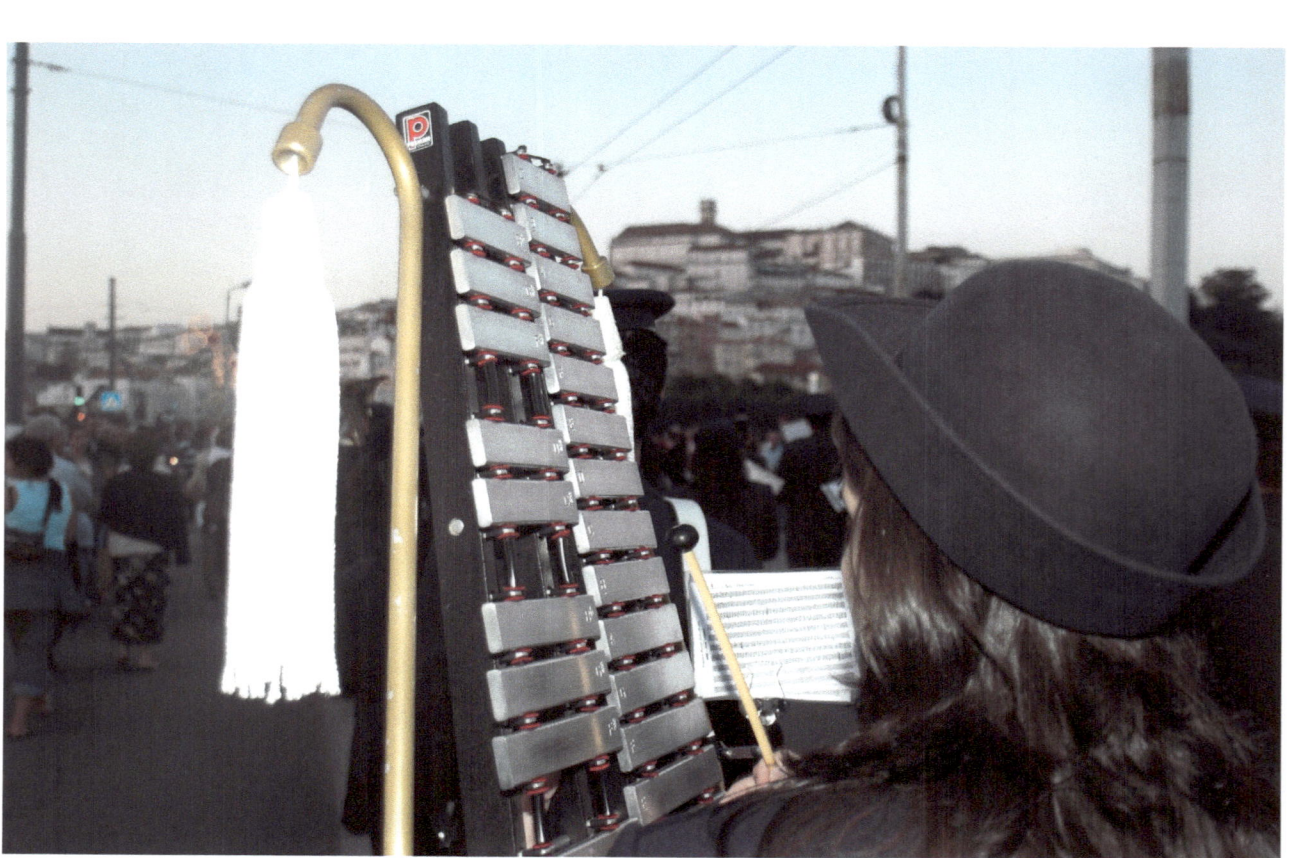

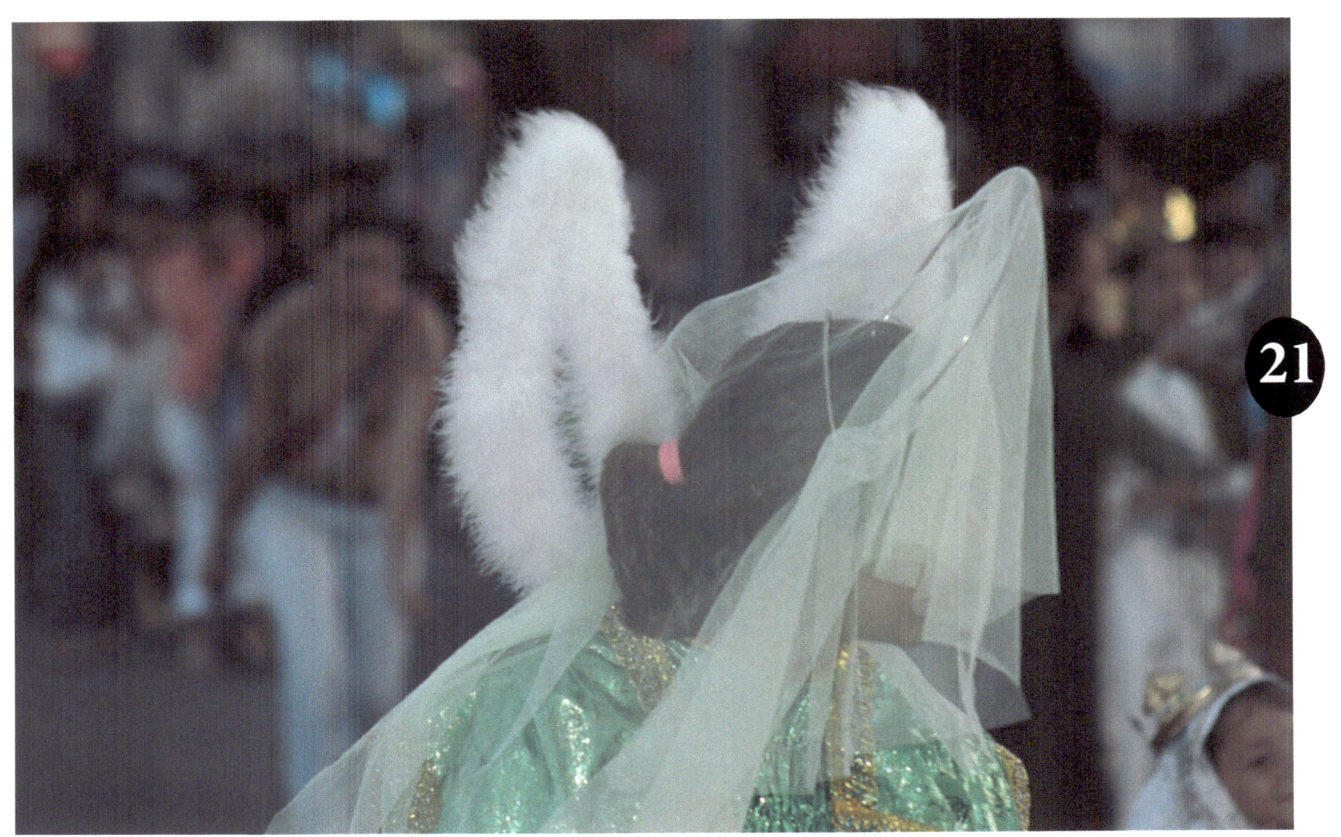

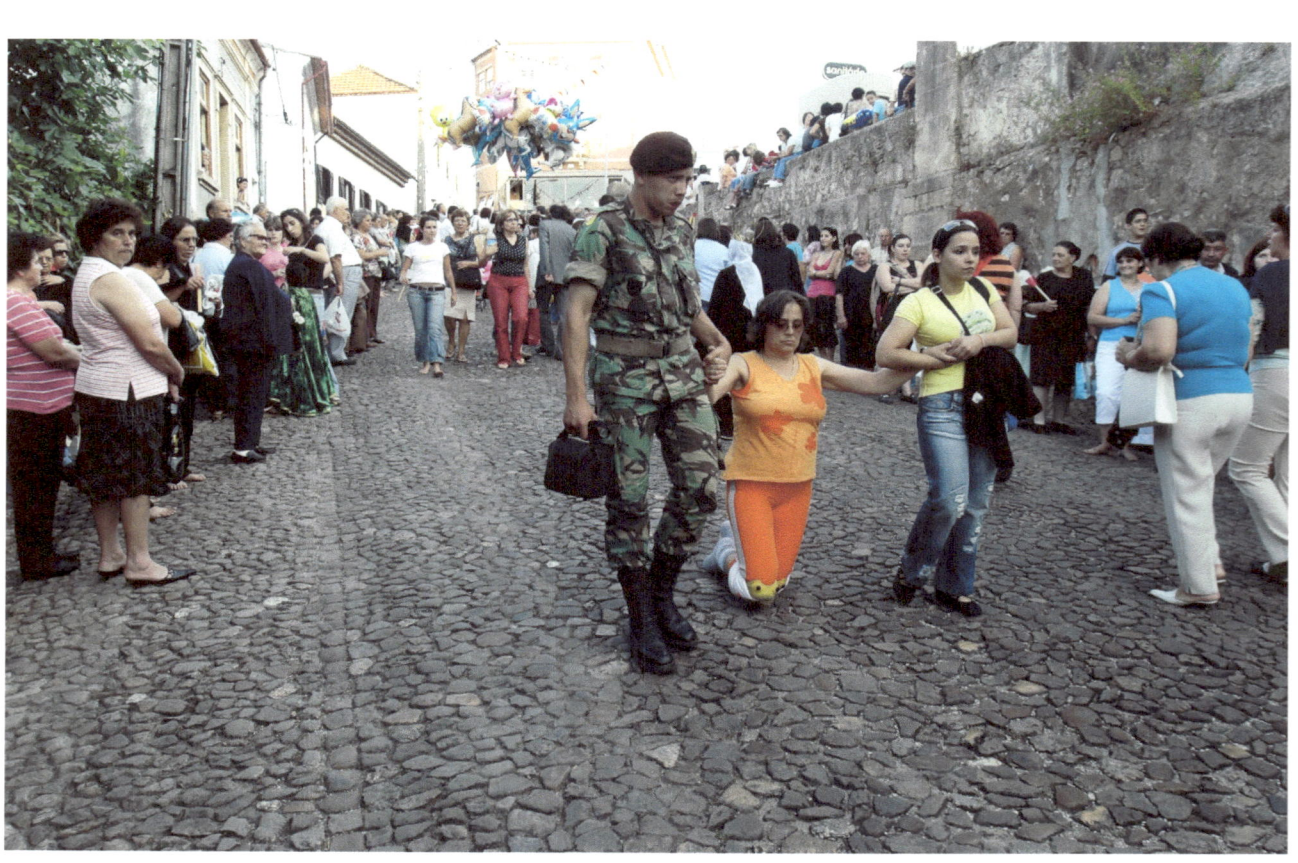

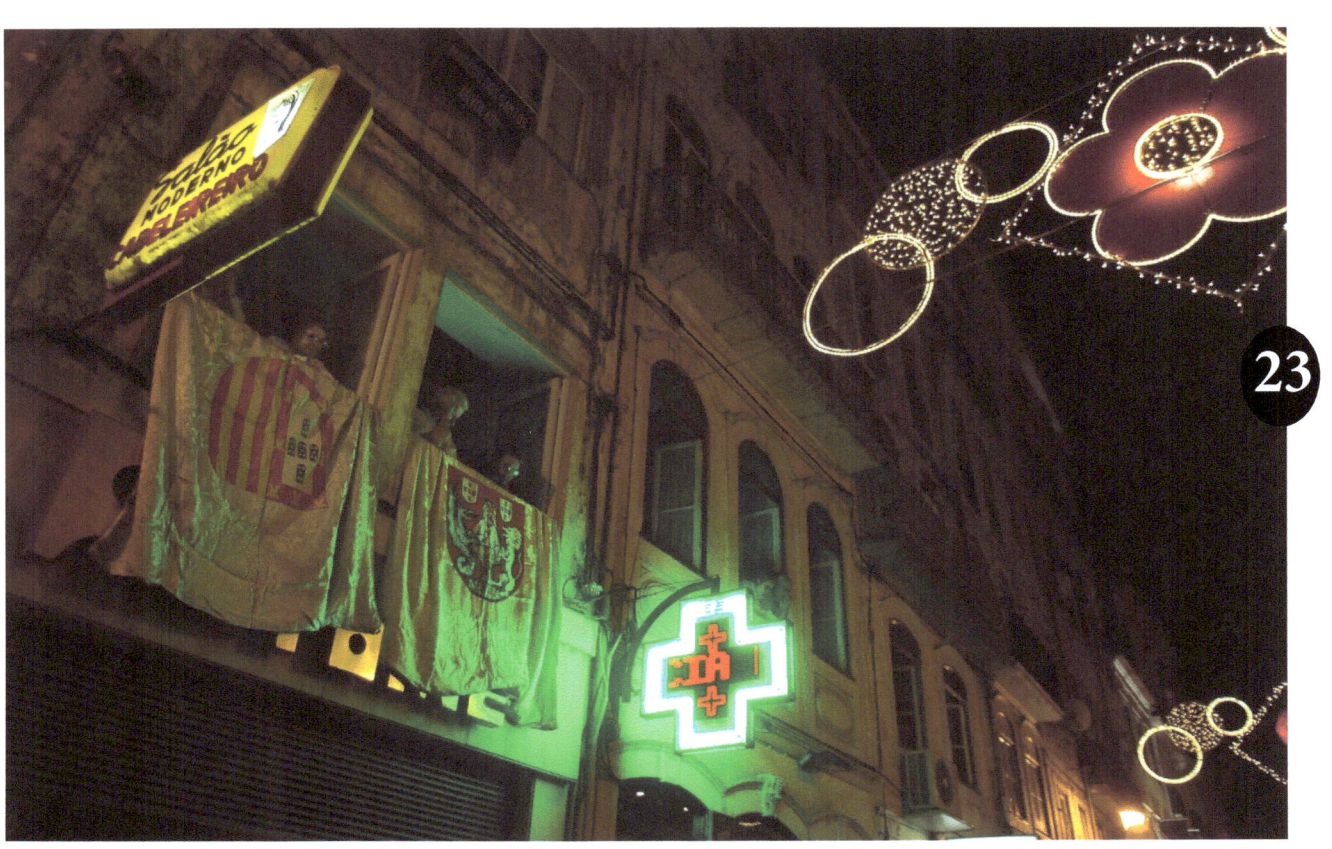

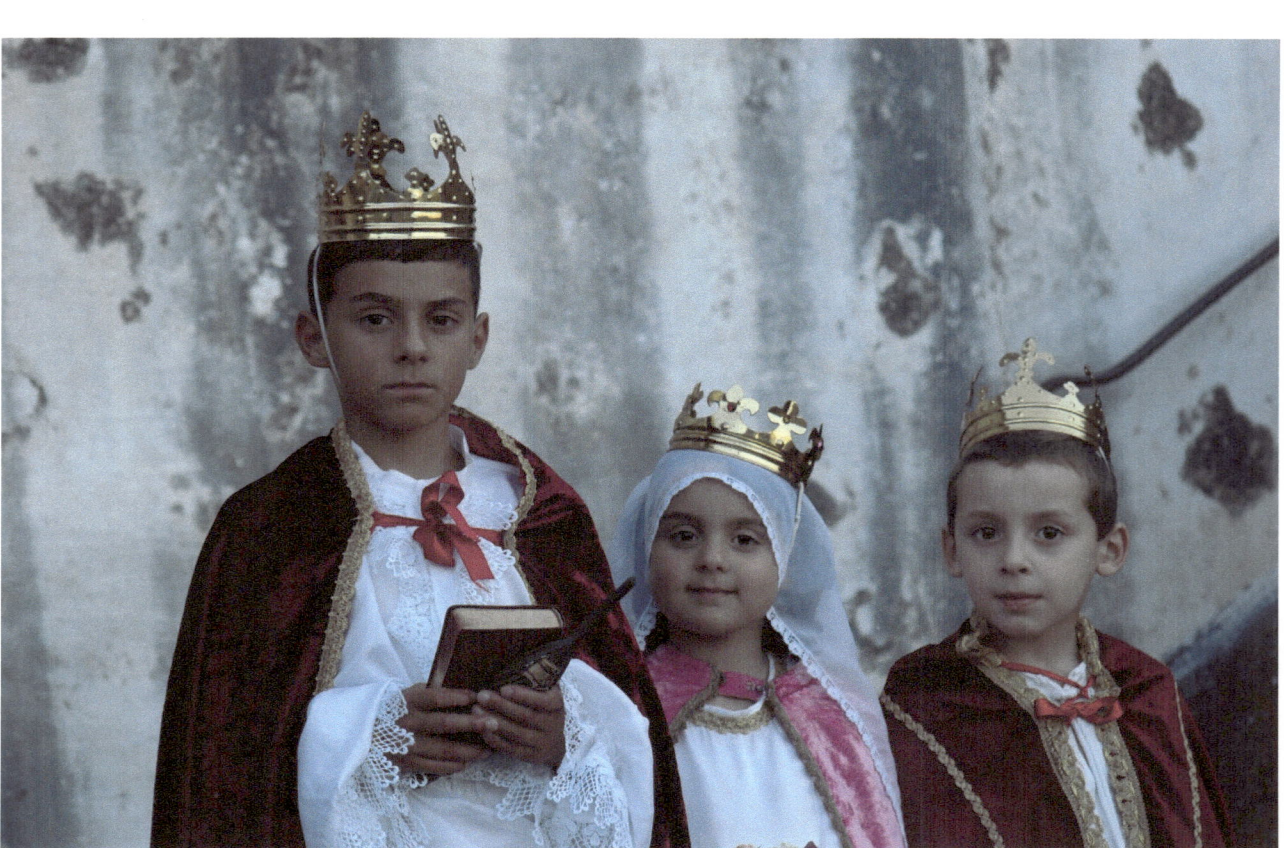

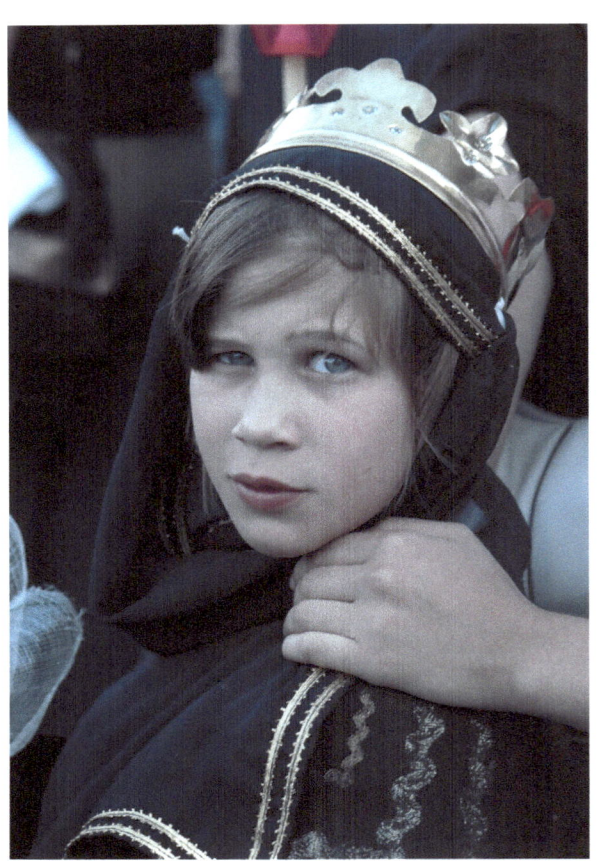
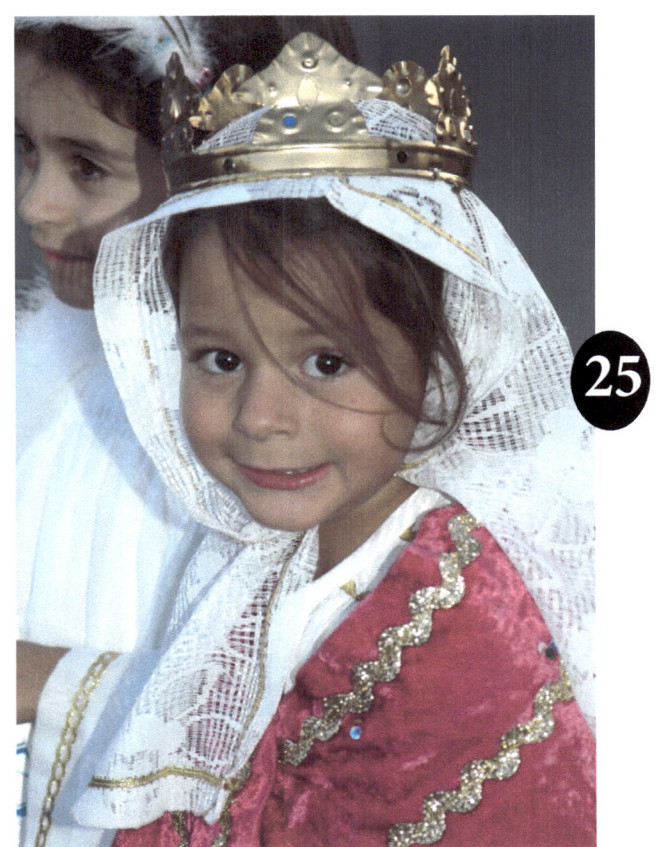

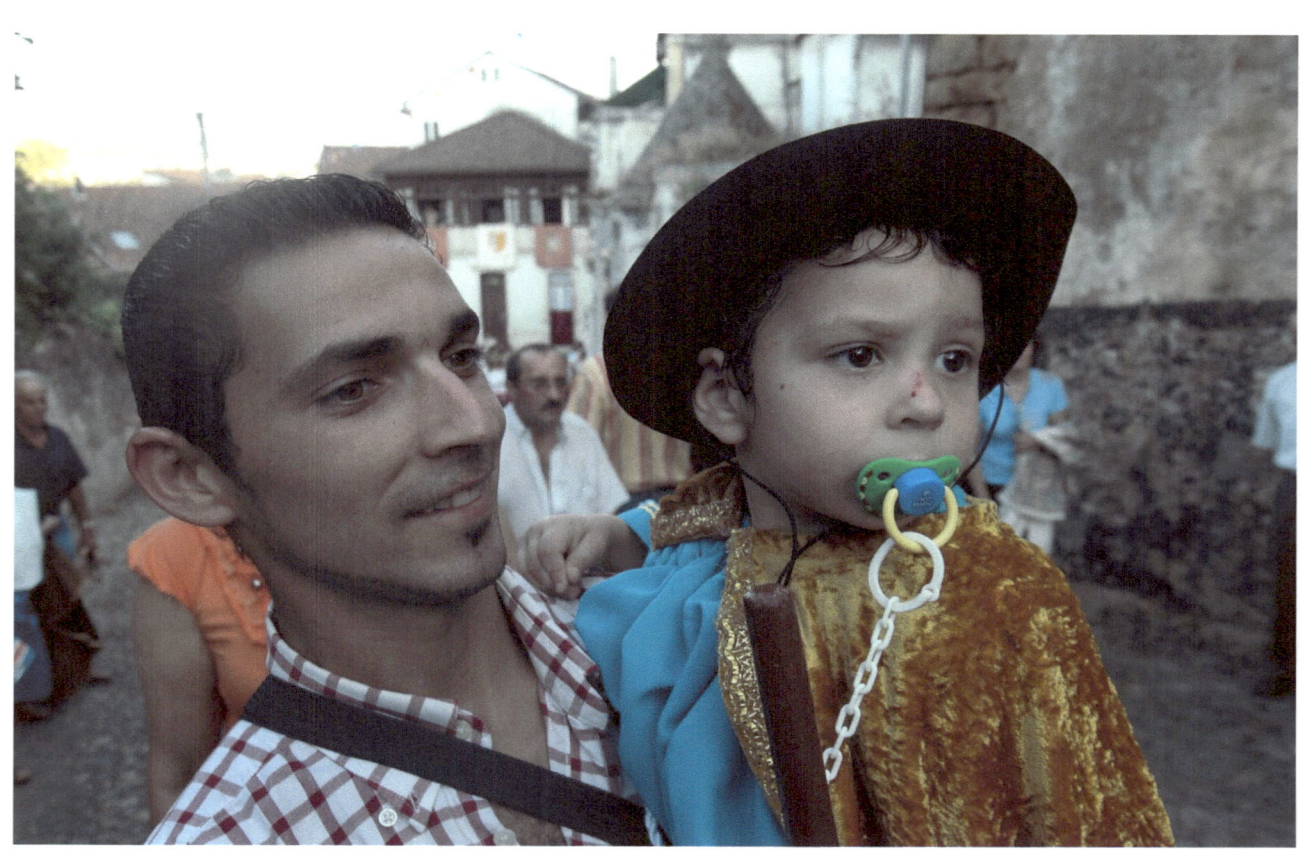

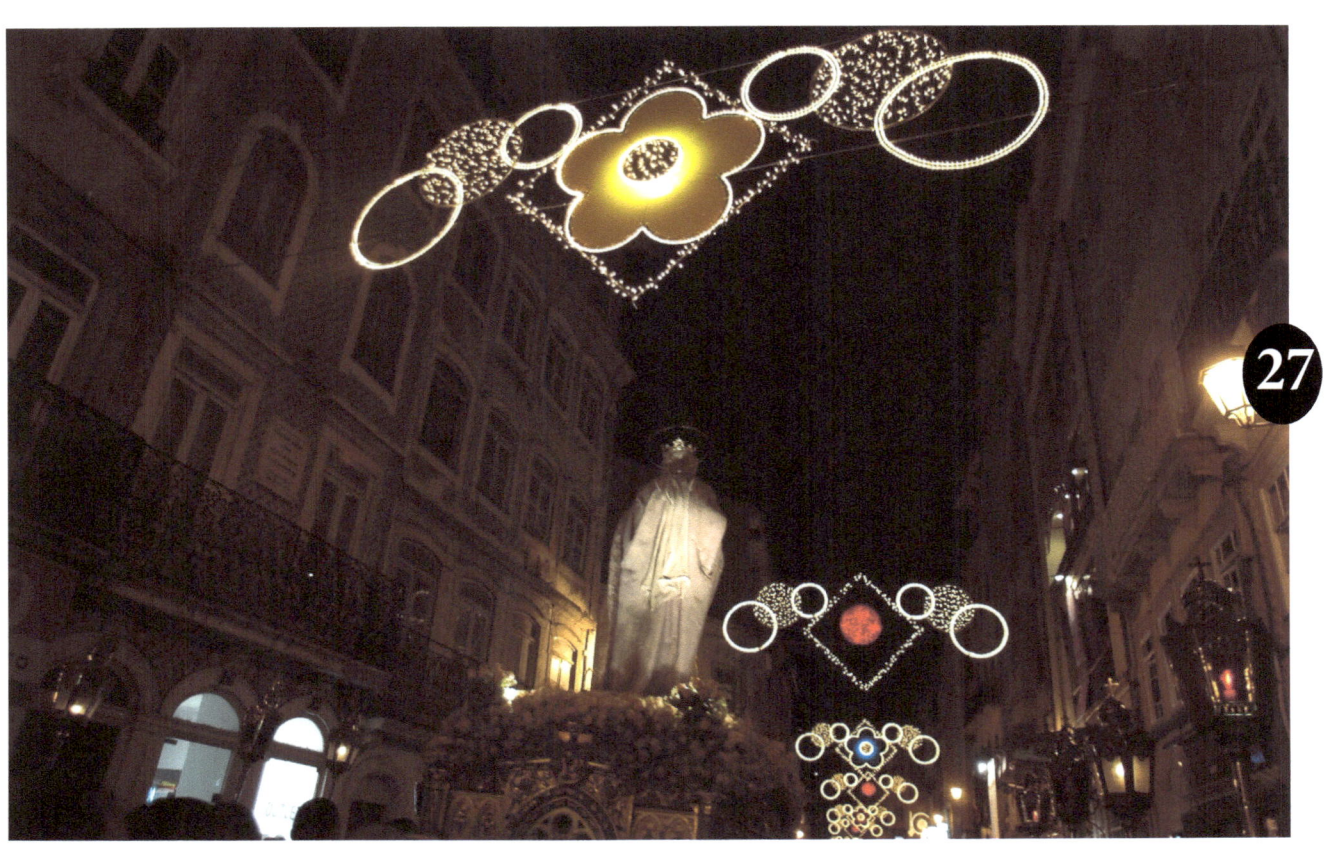

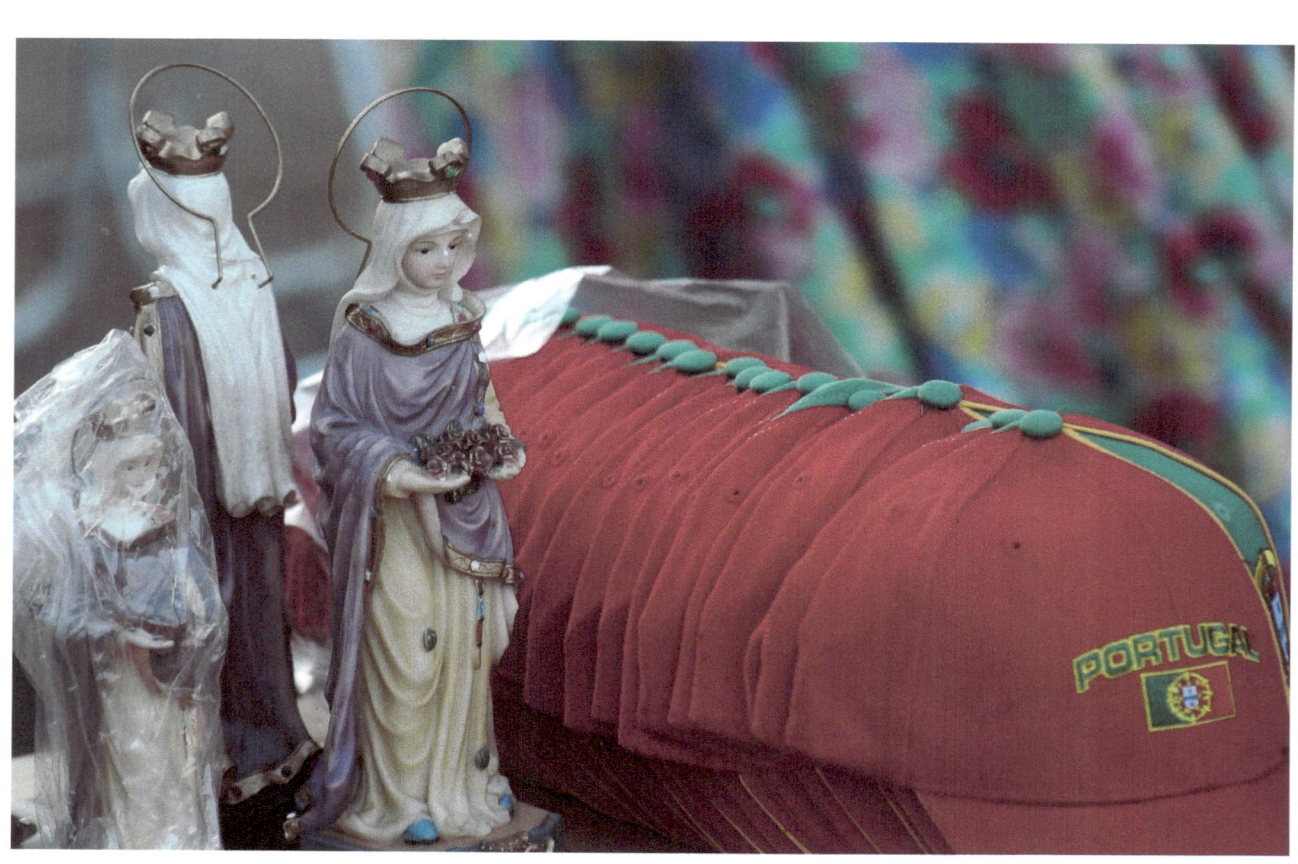

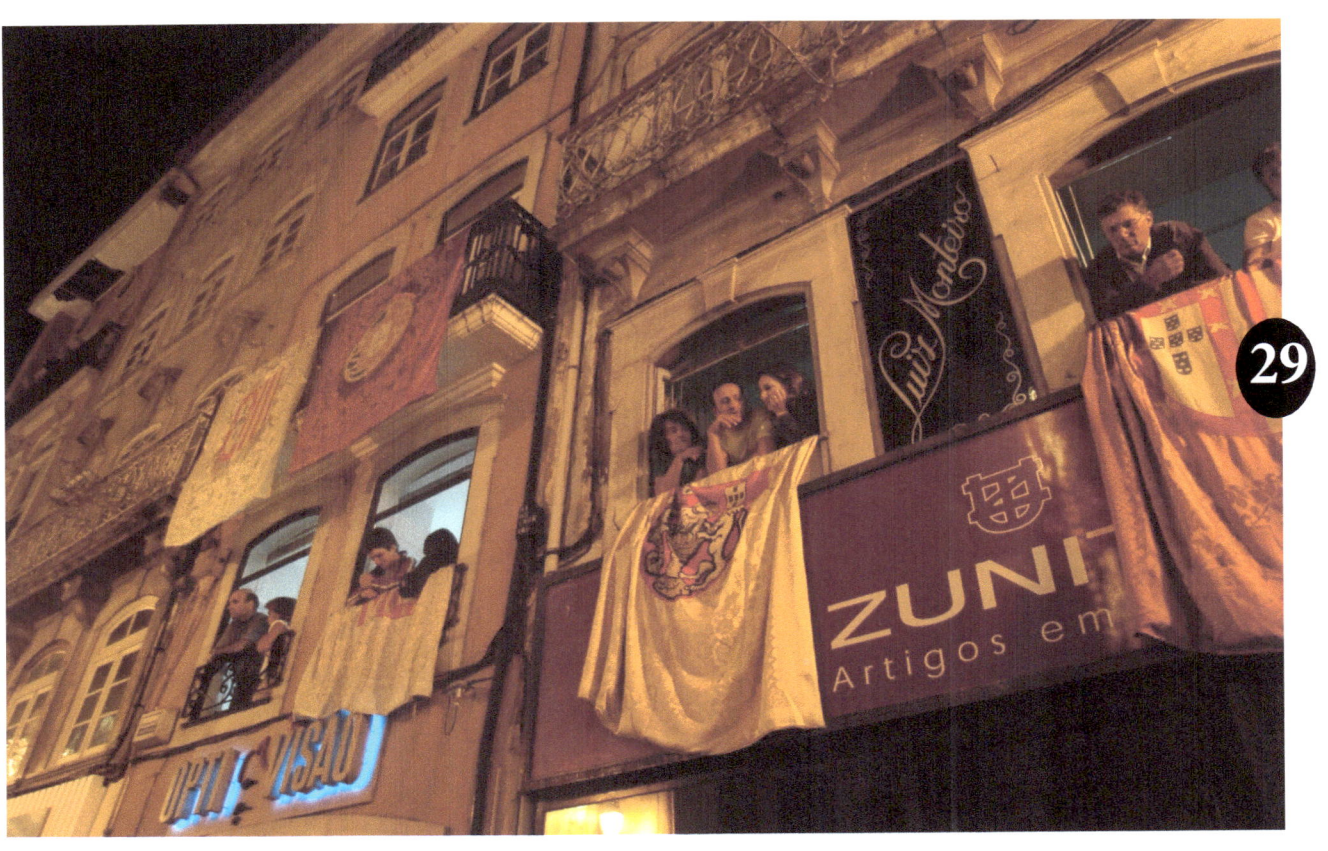

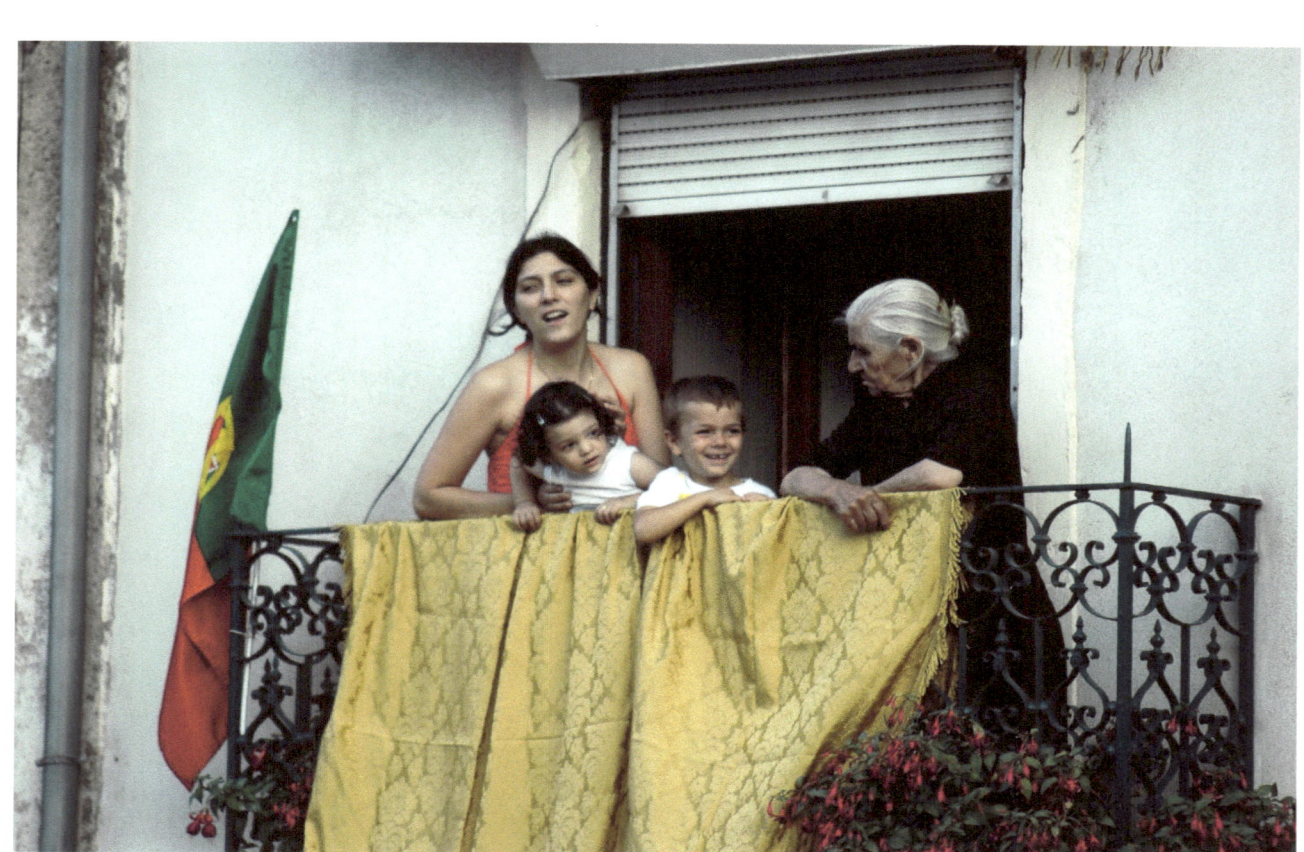

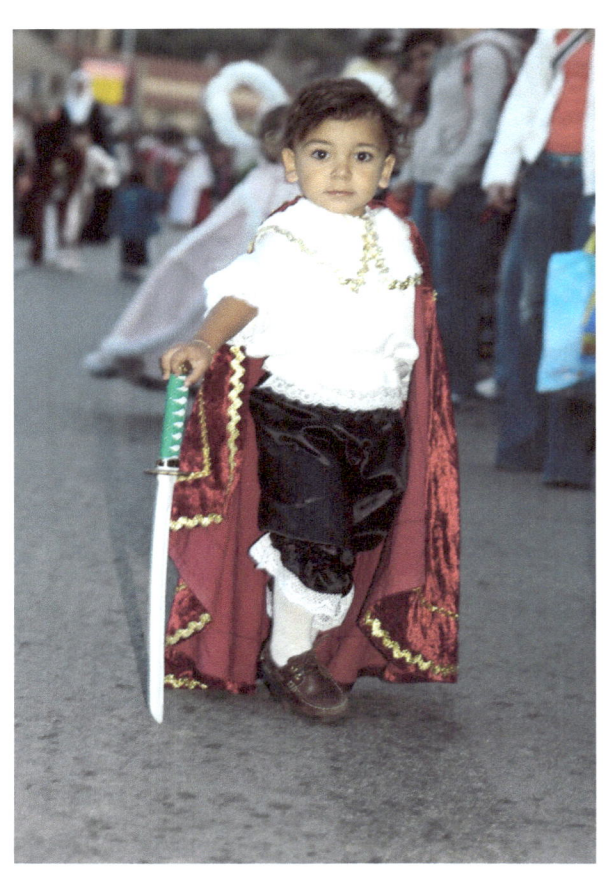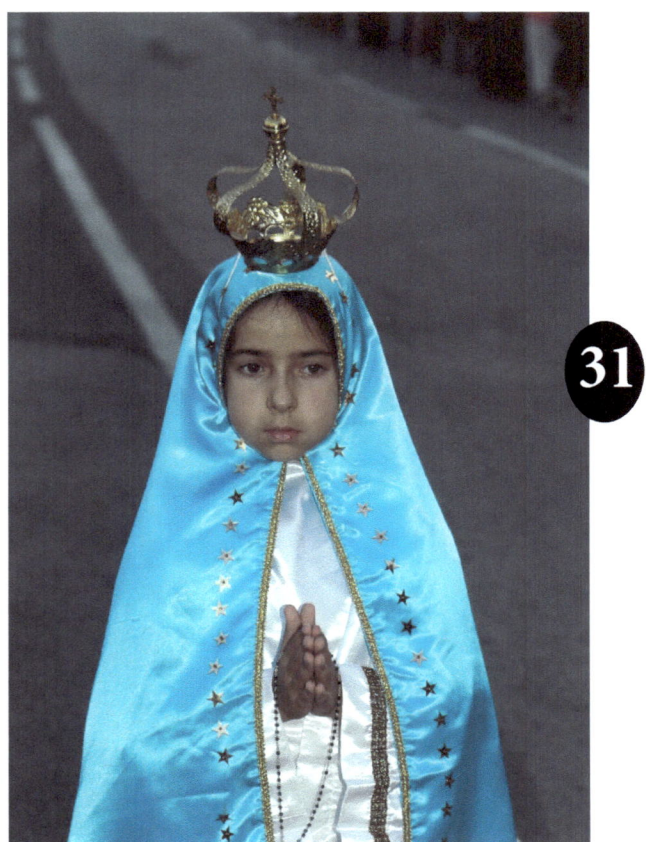

31

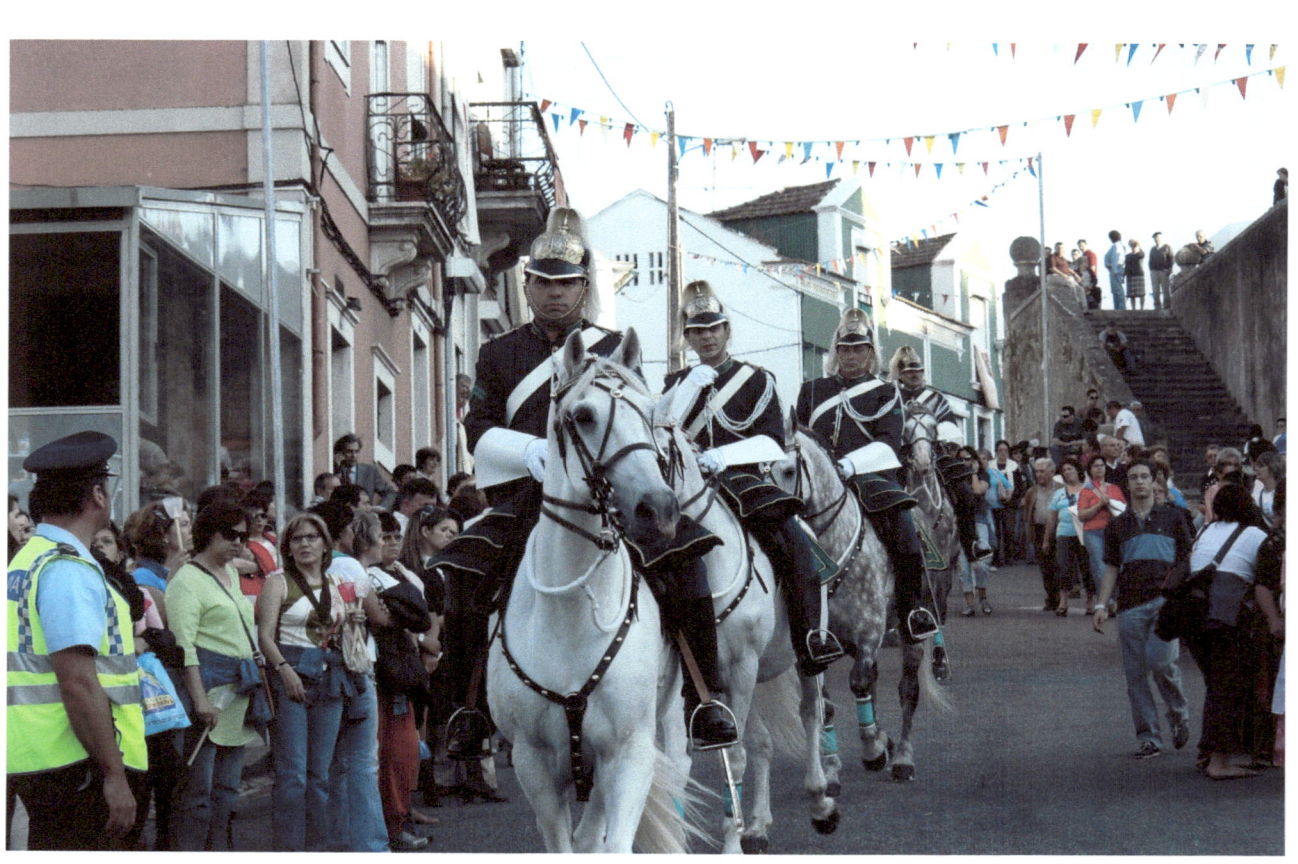

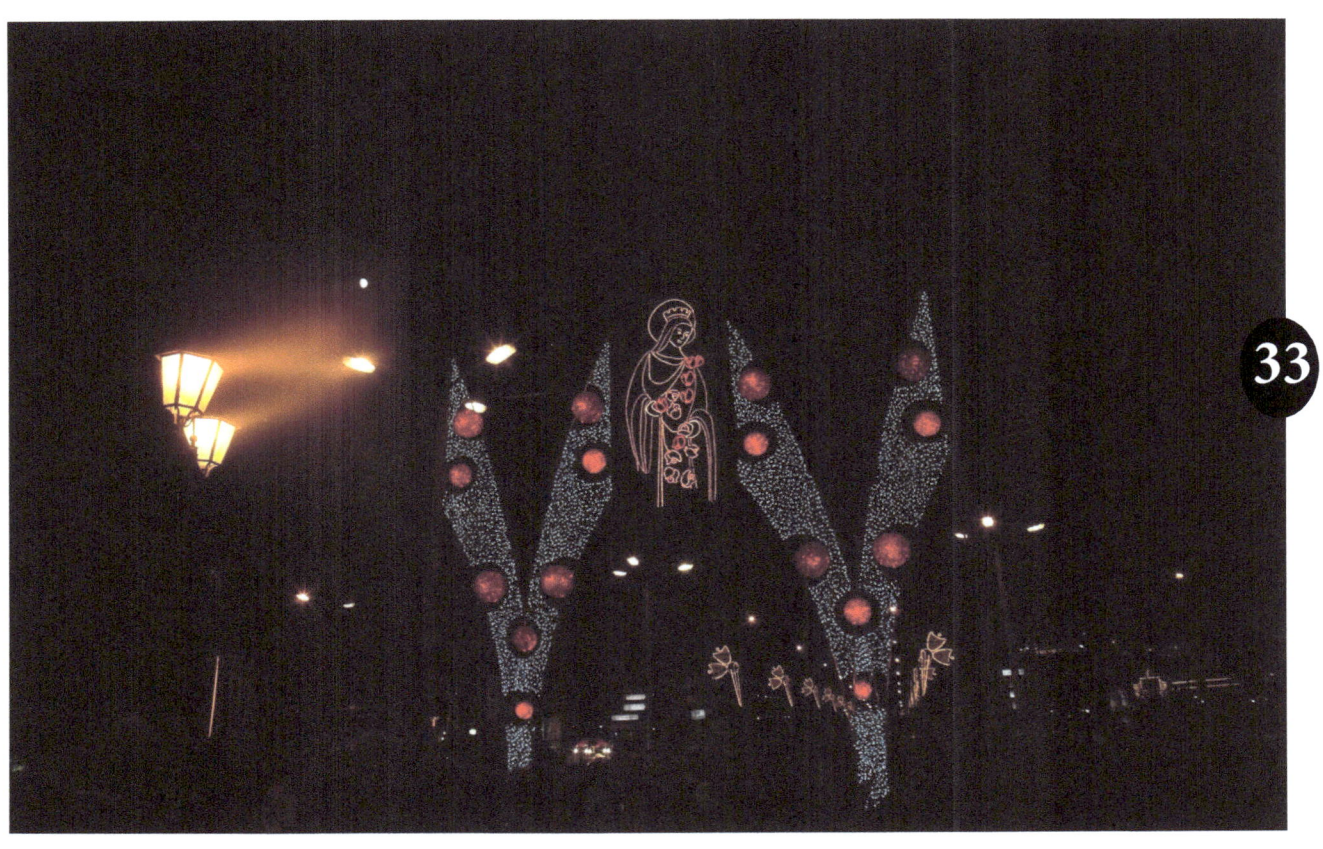

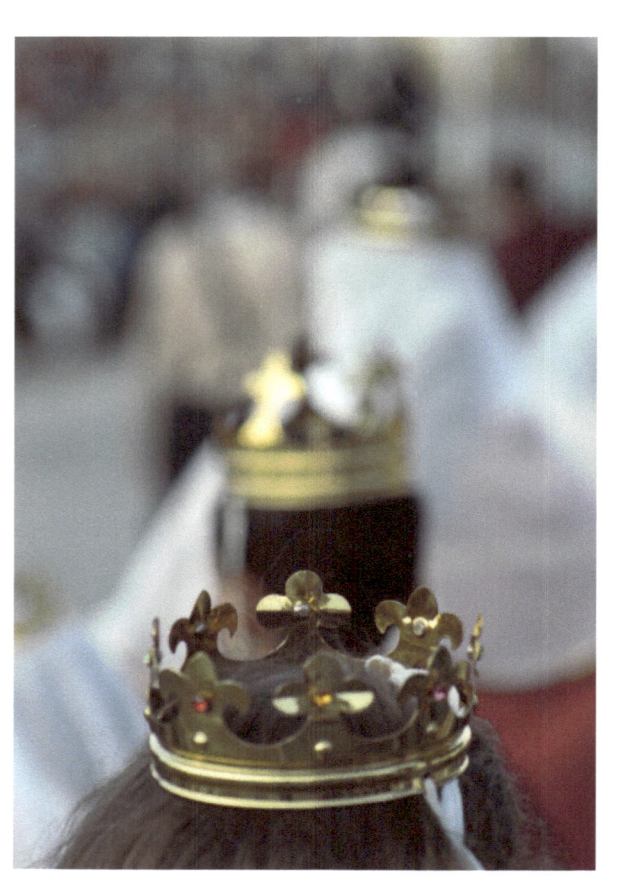 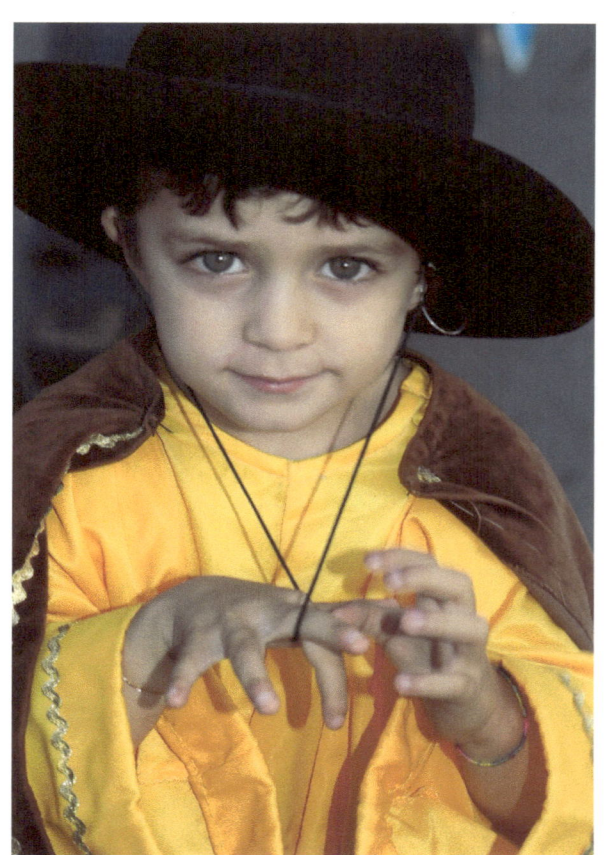

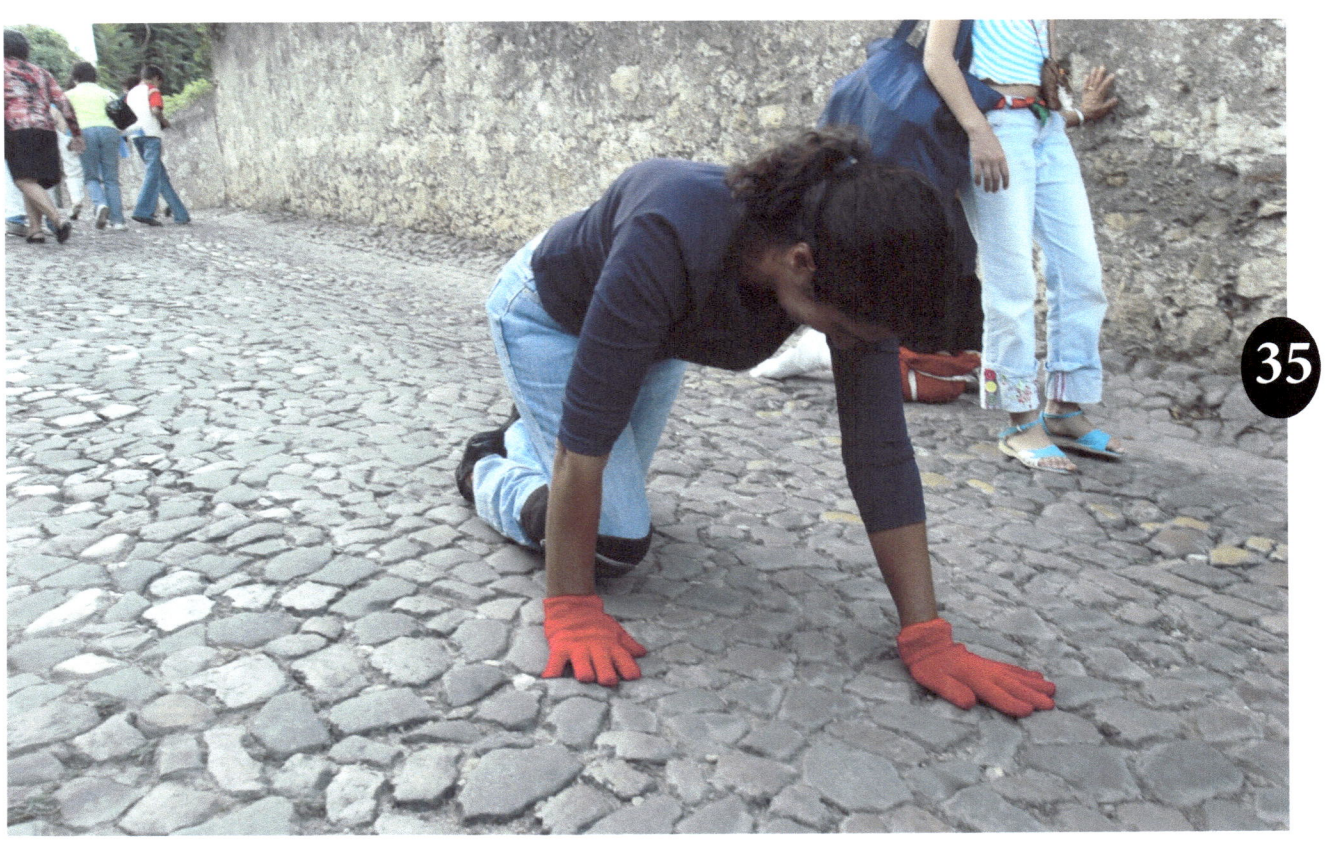

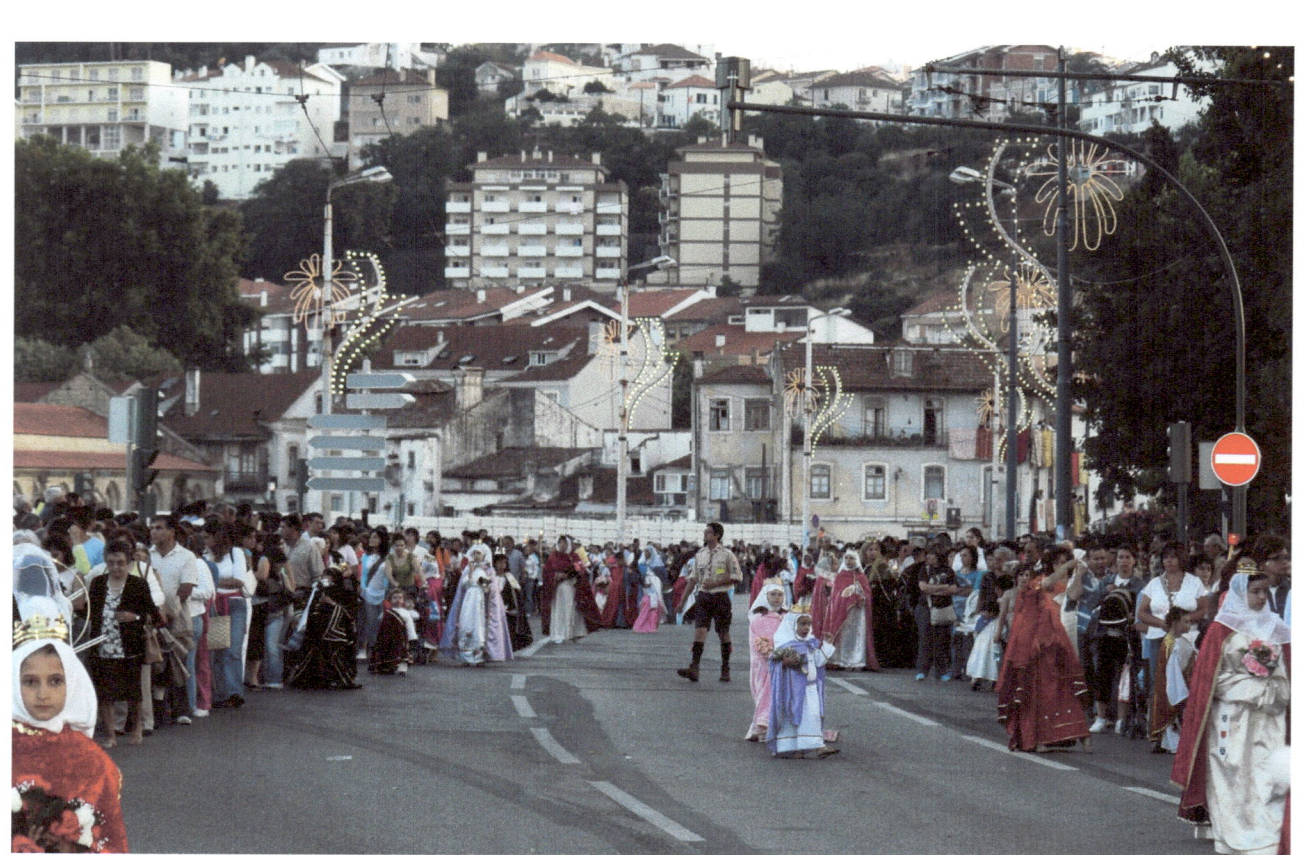

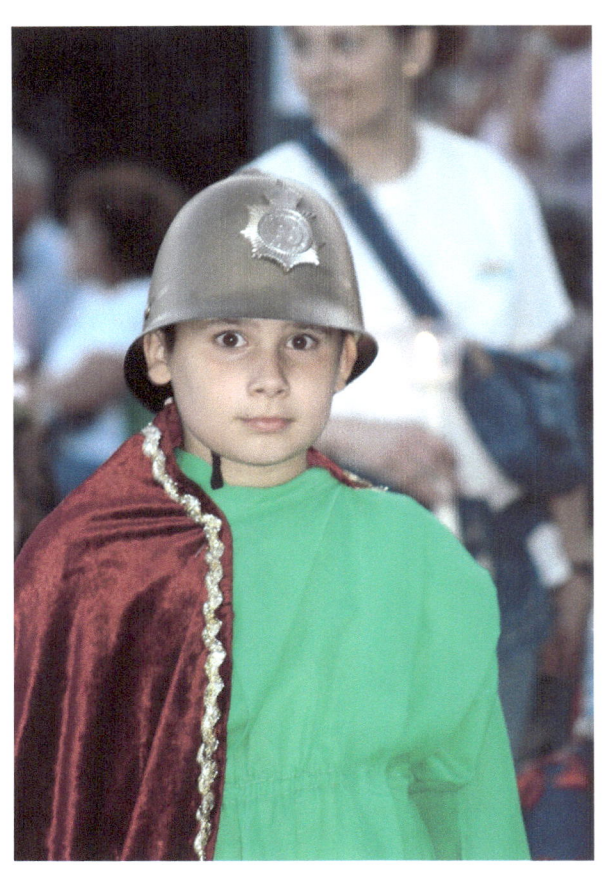
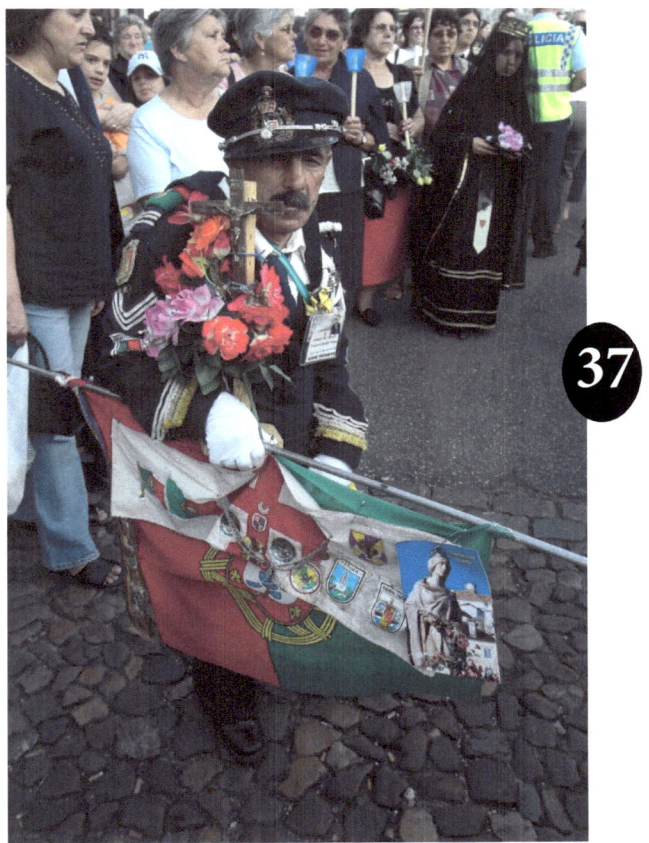

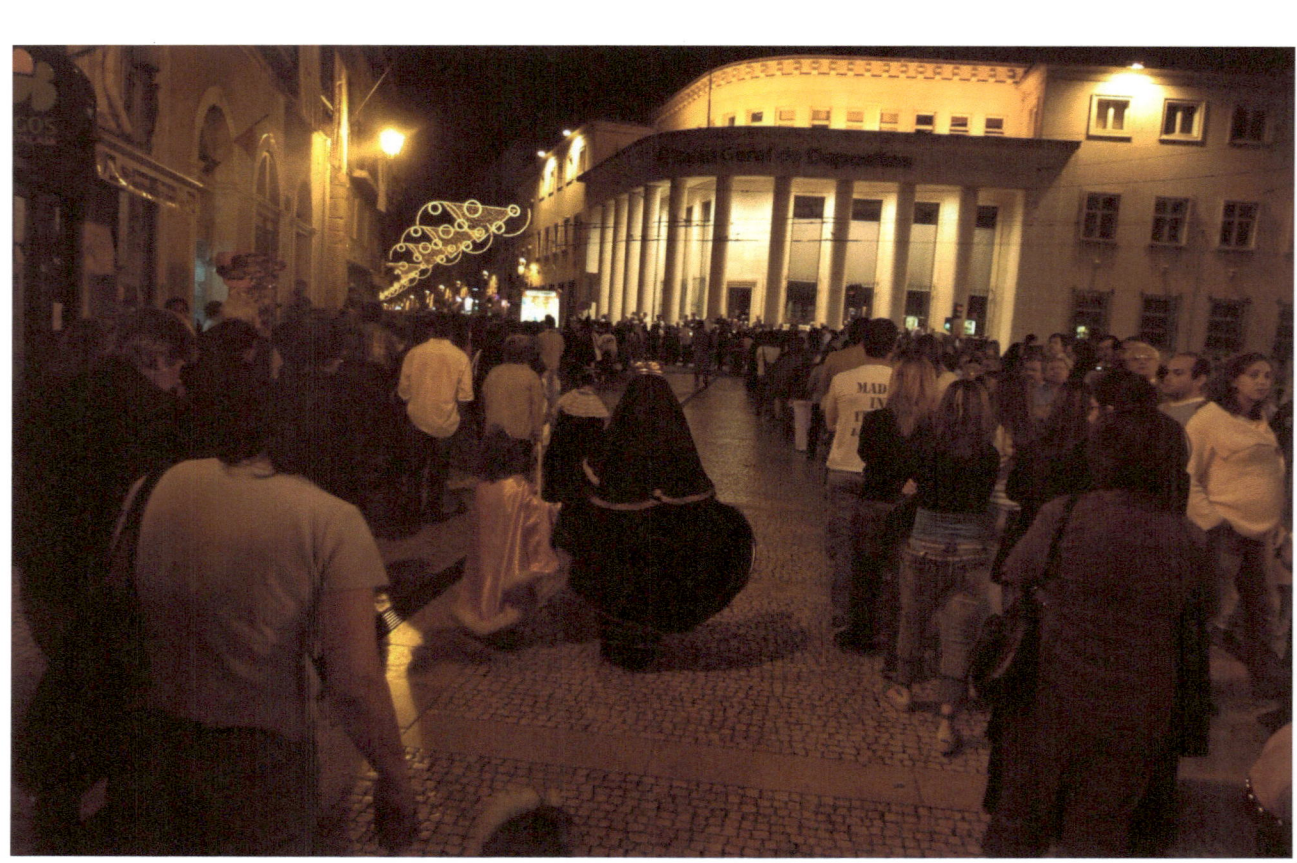

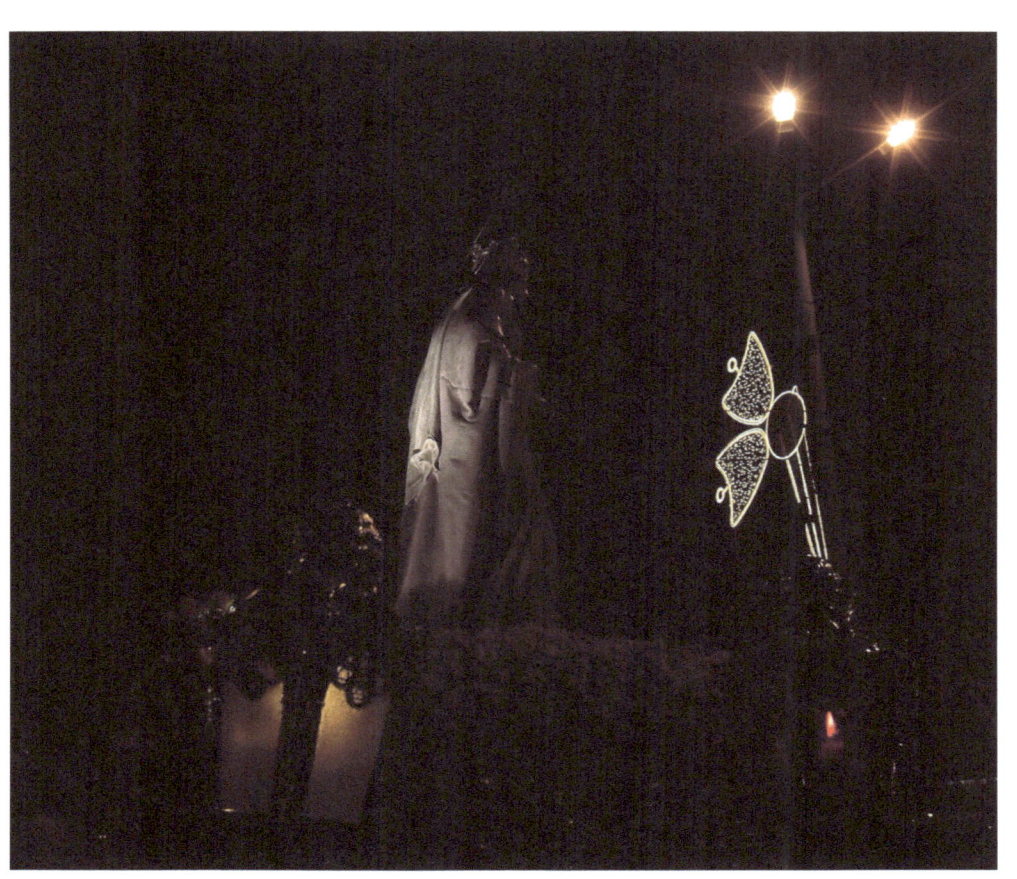

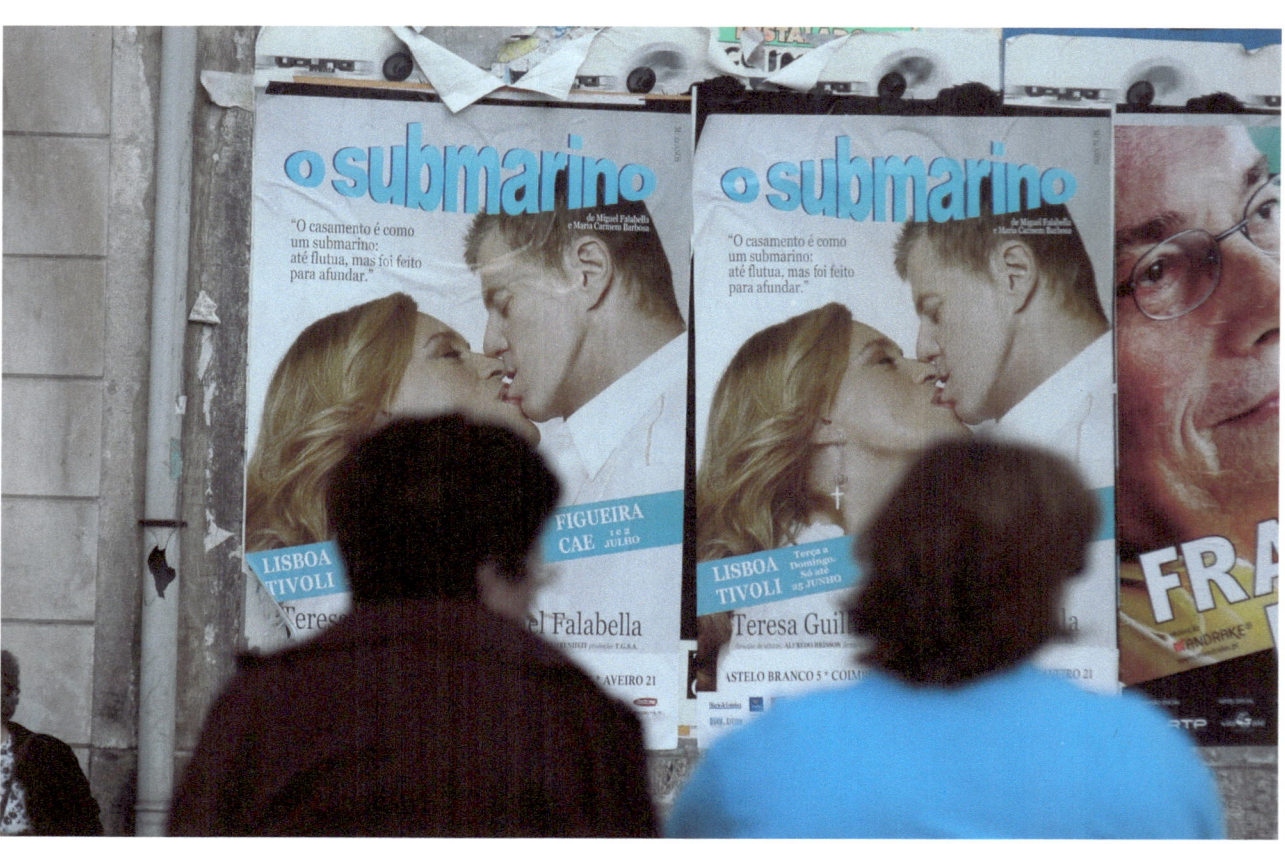

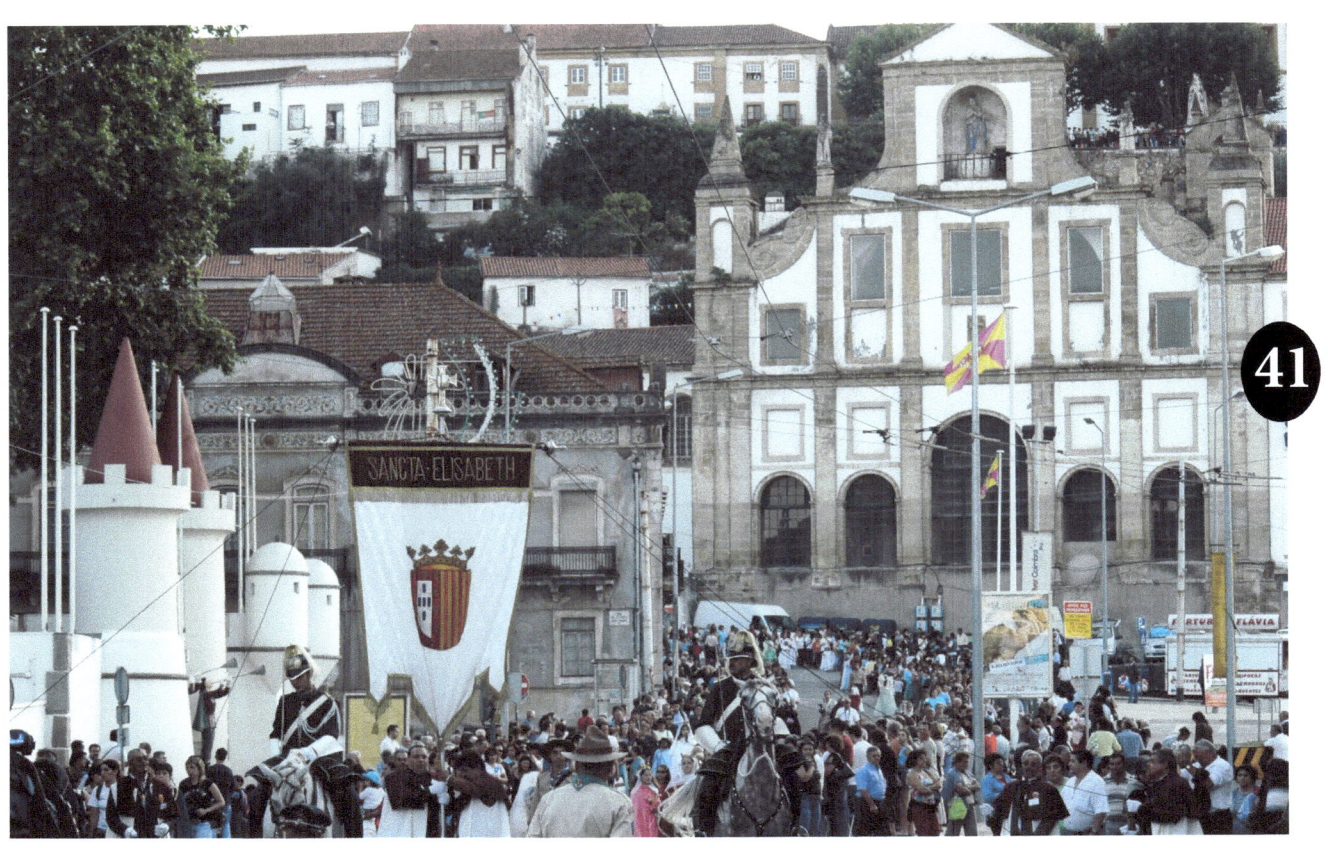

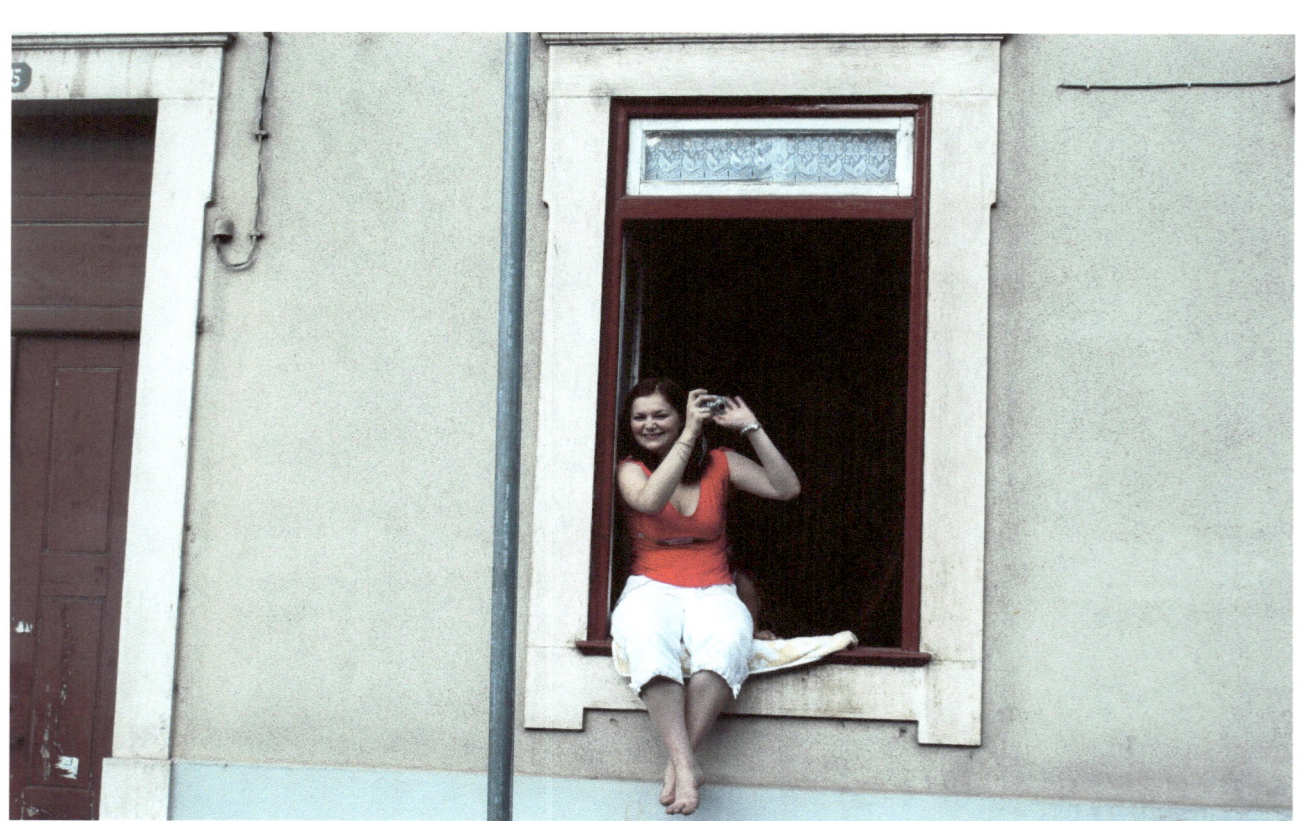

43

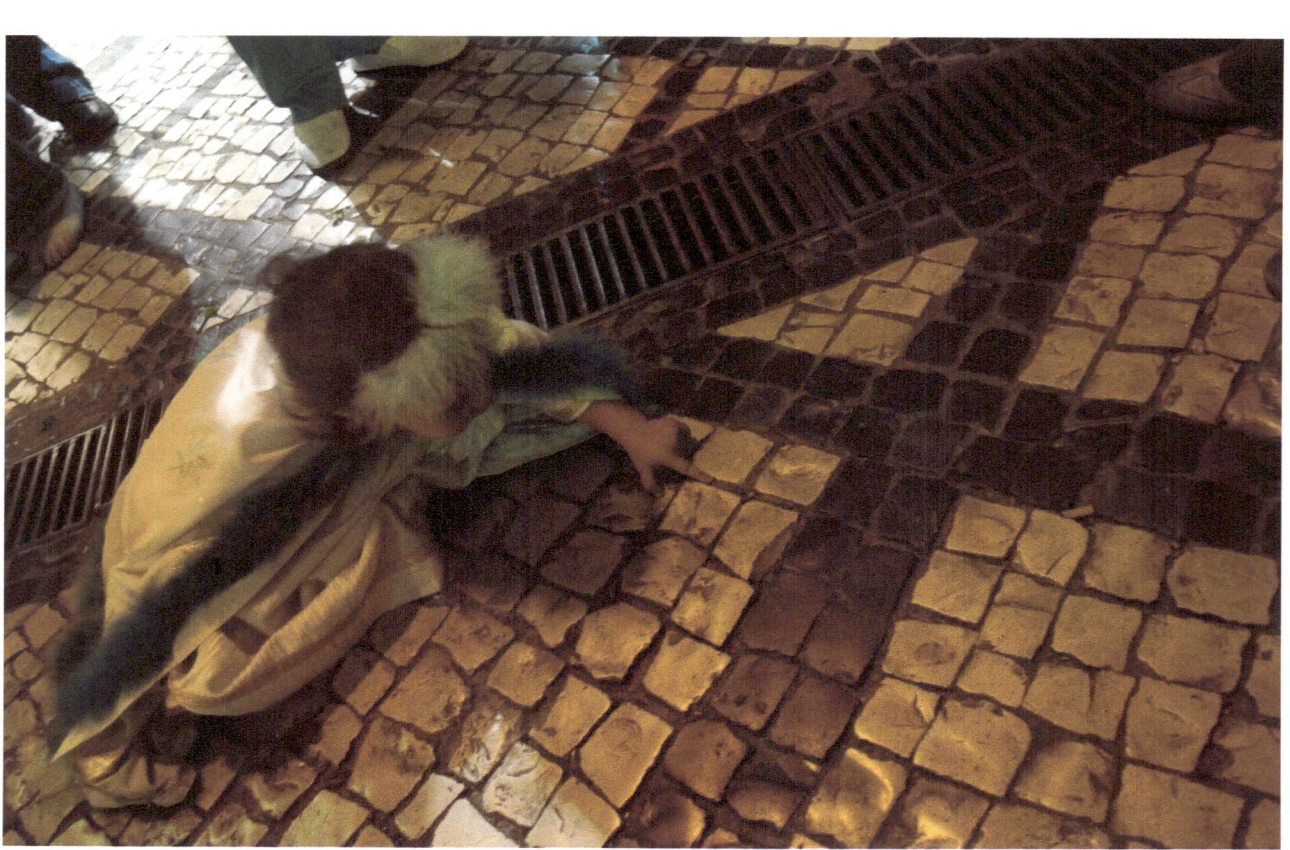

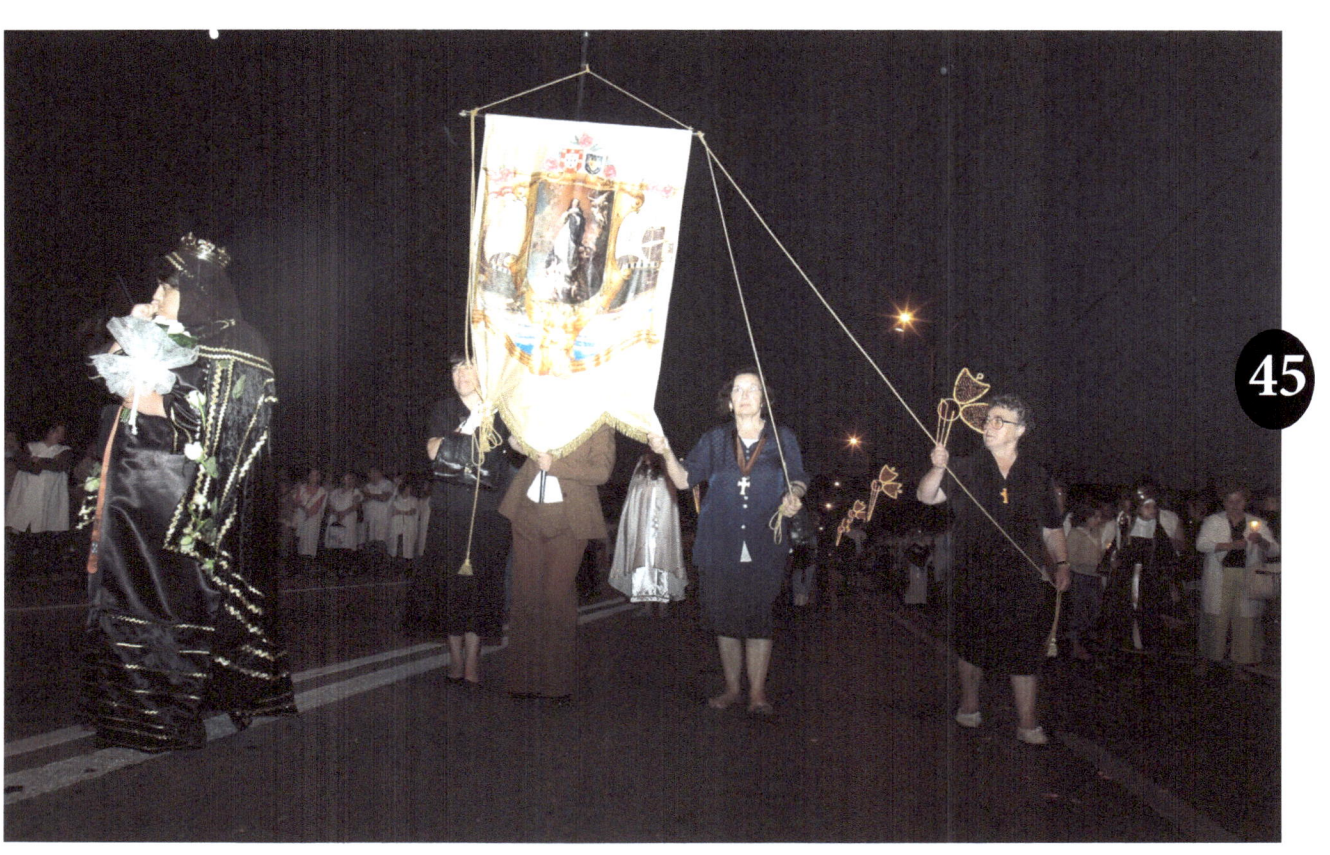

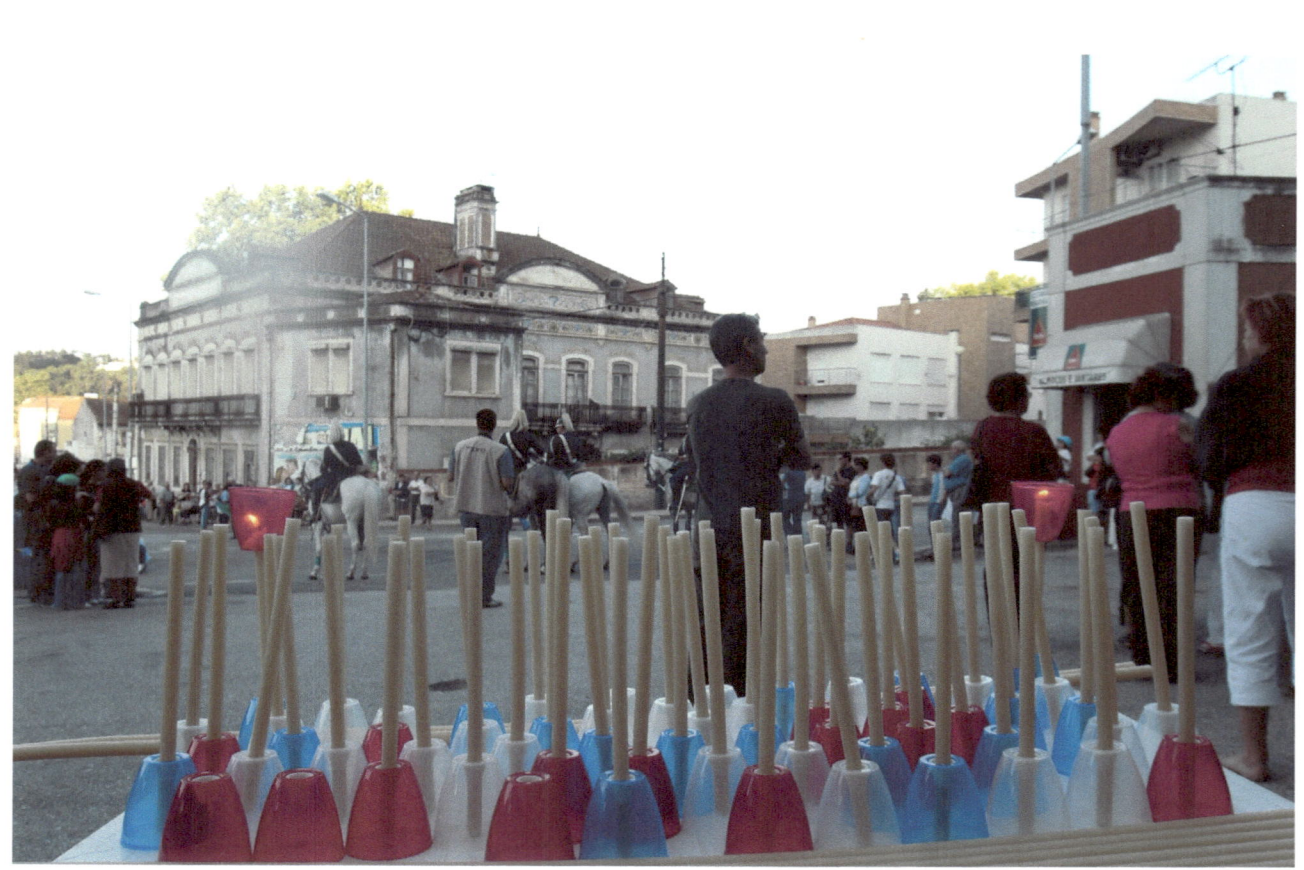

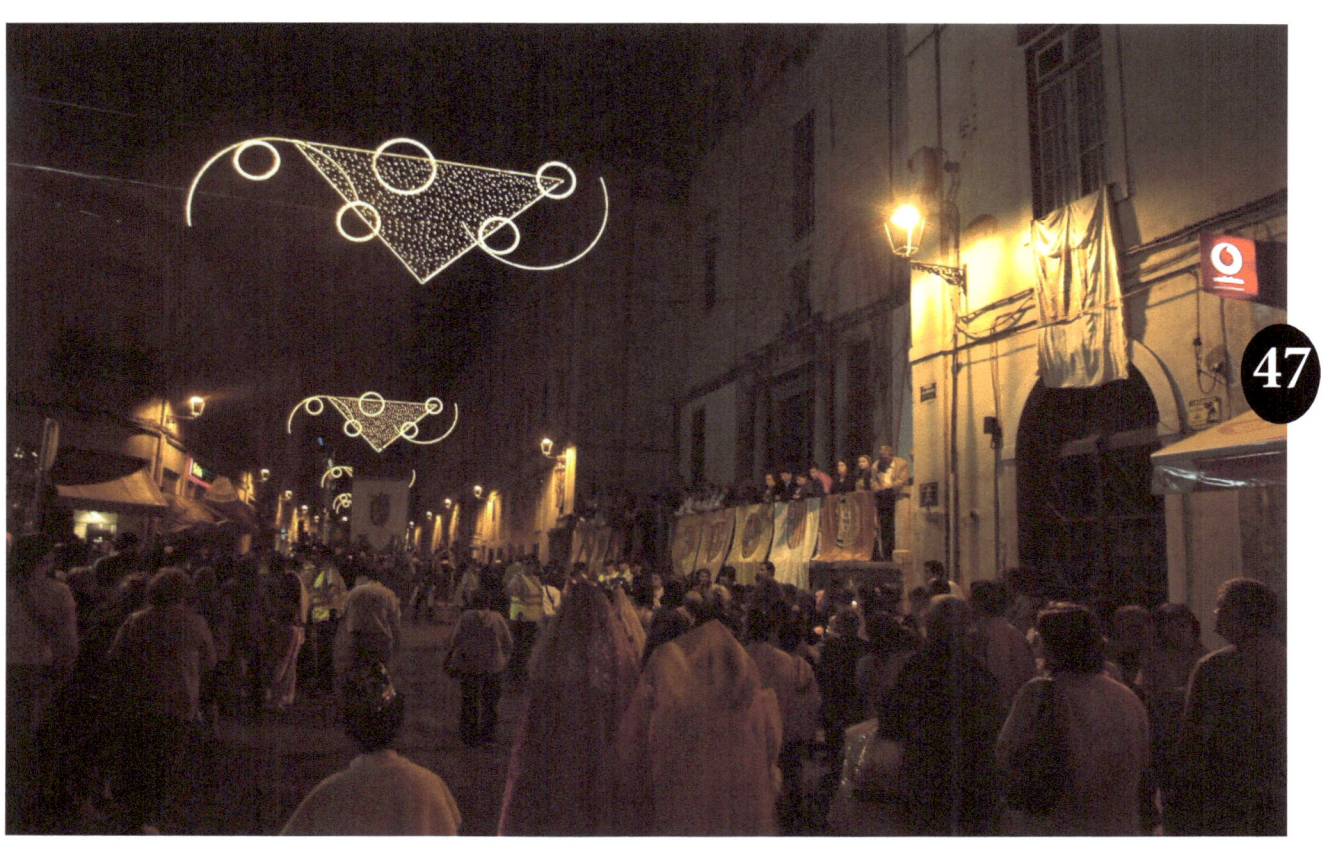

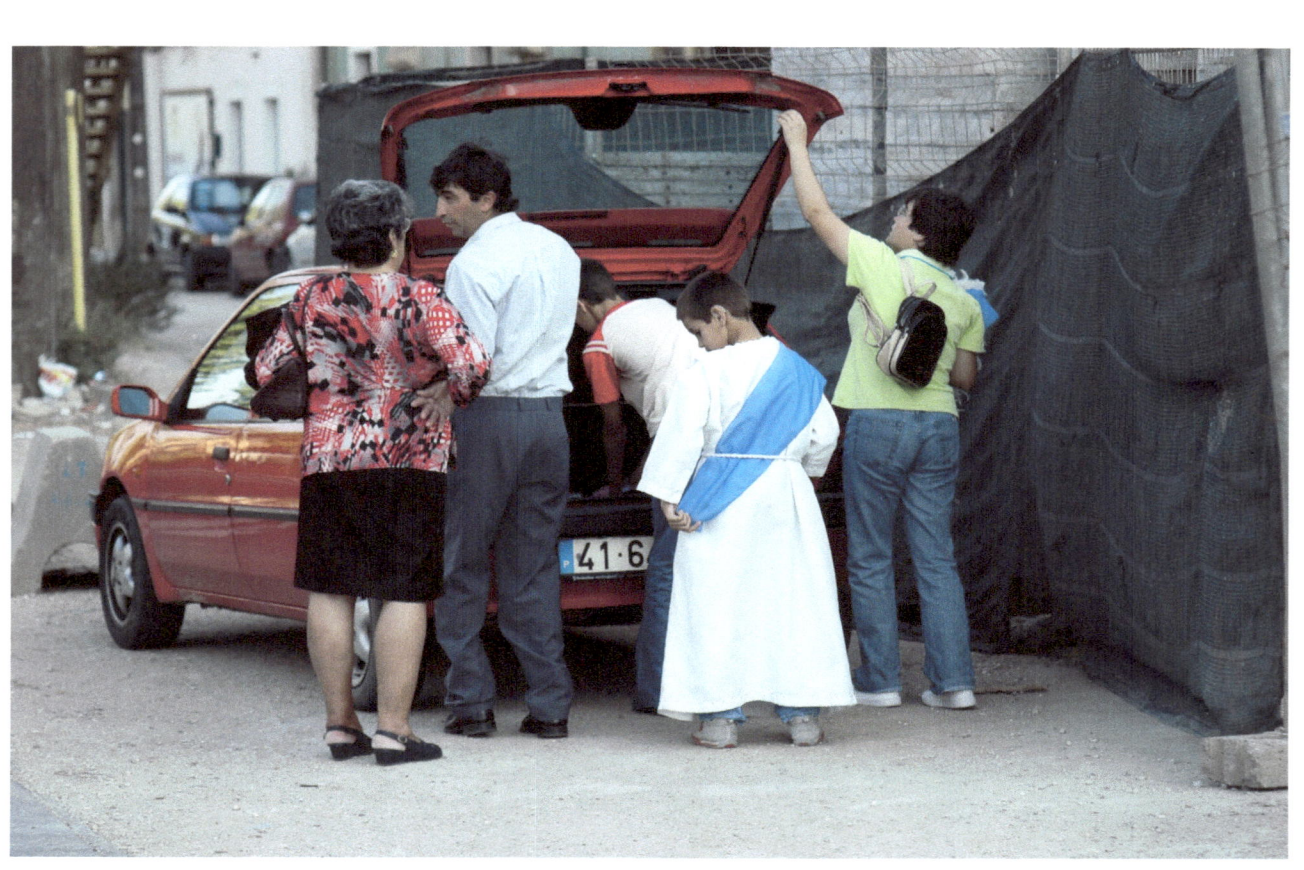

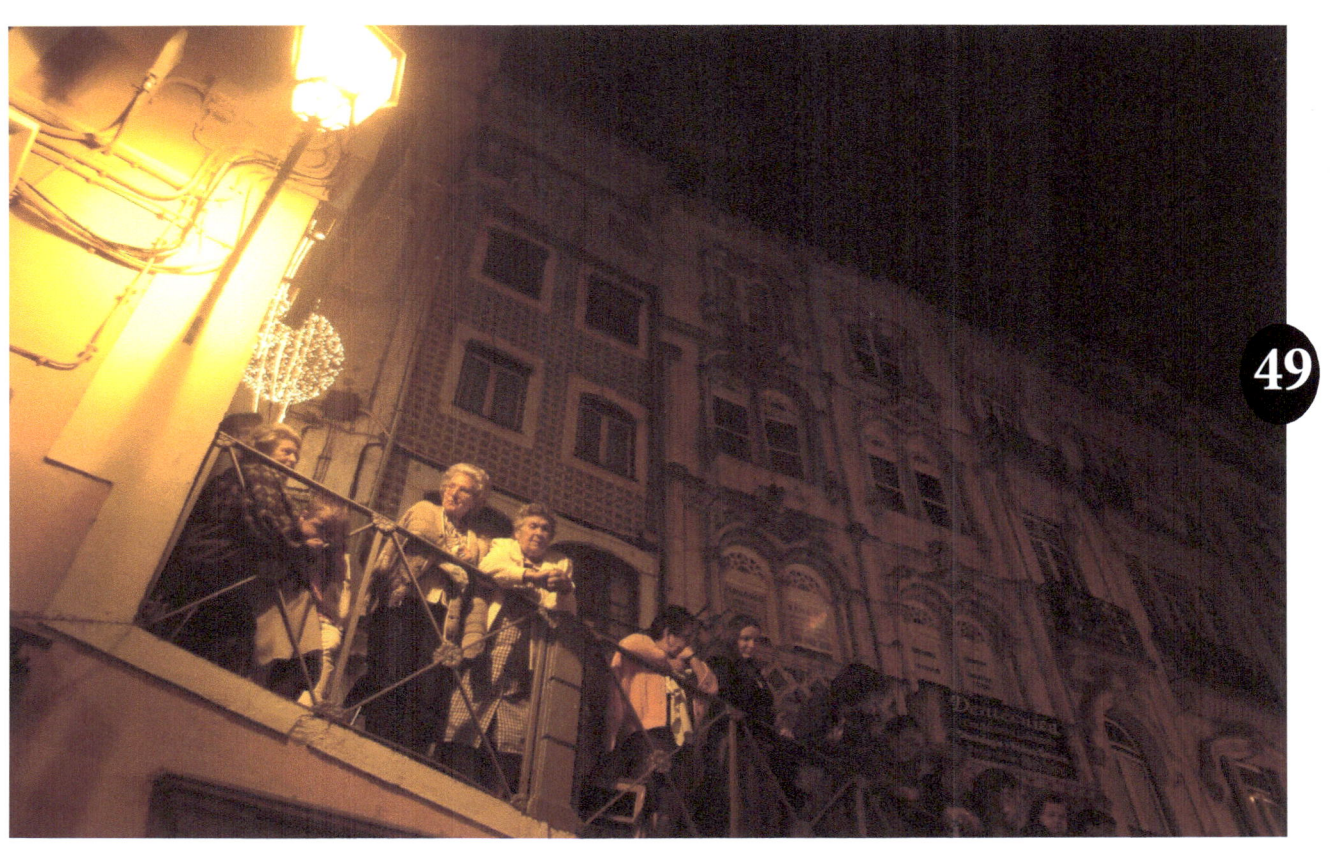

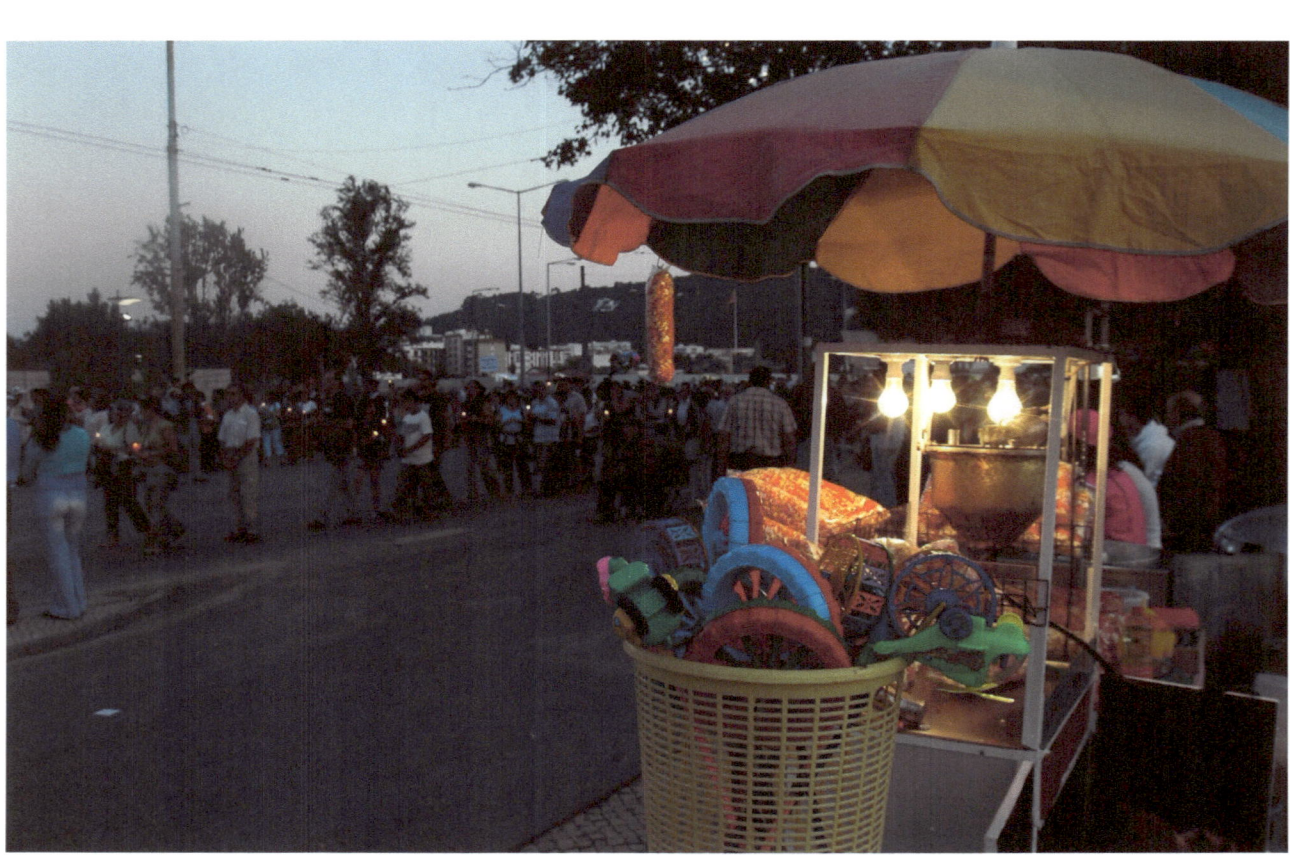

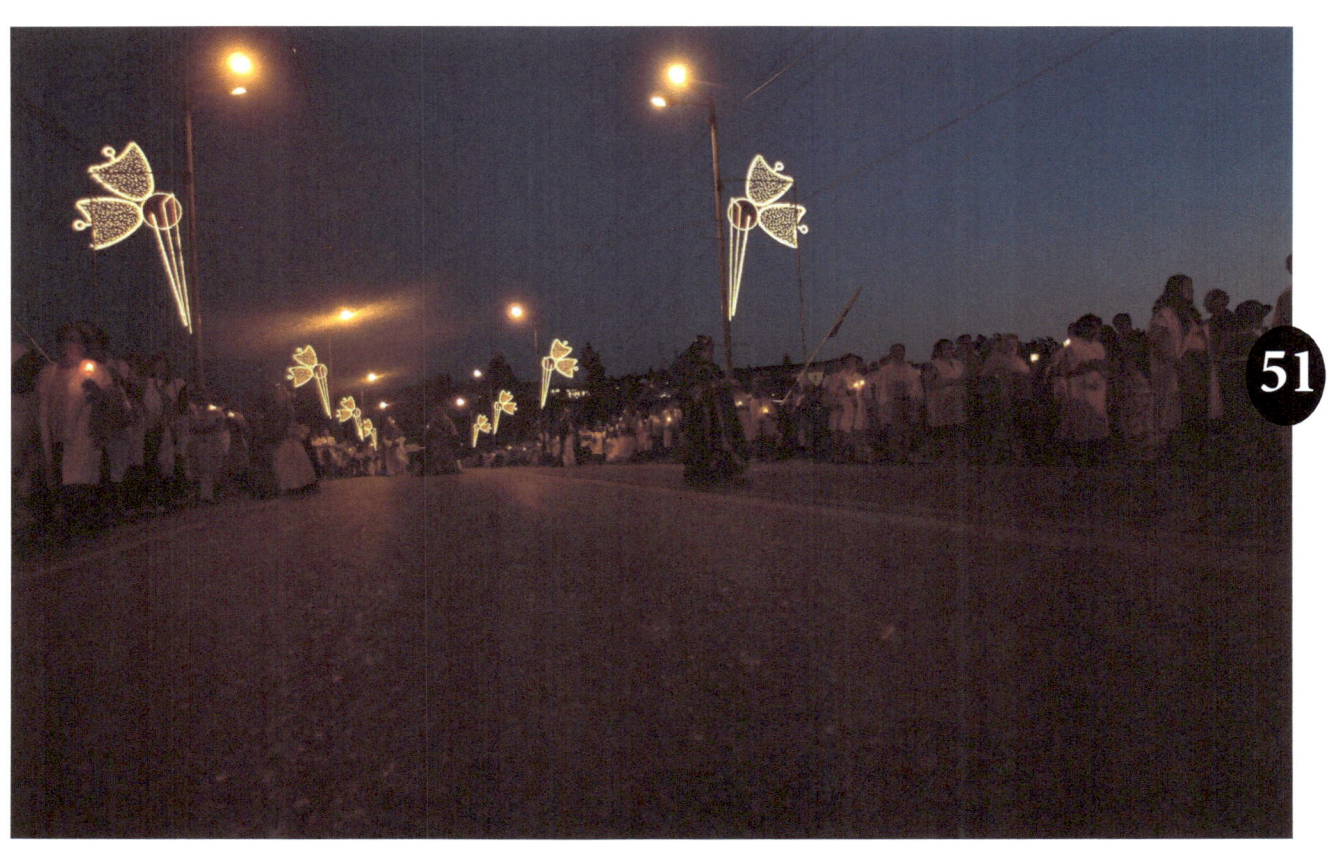

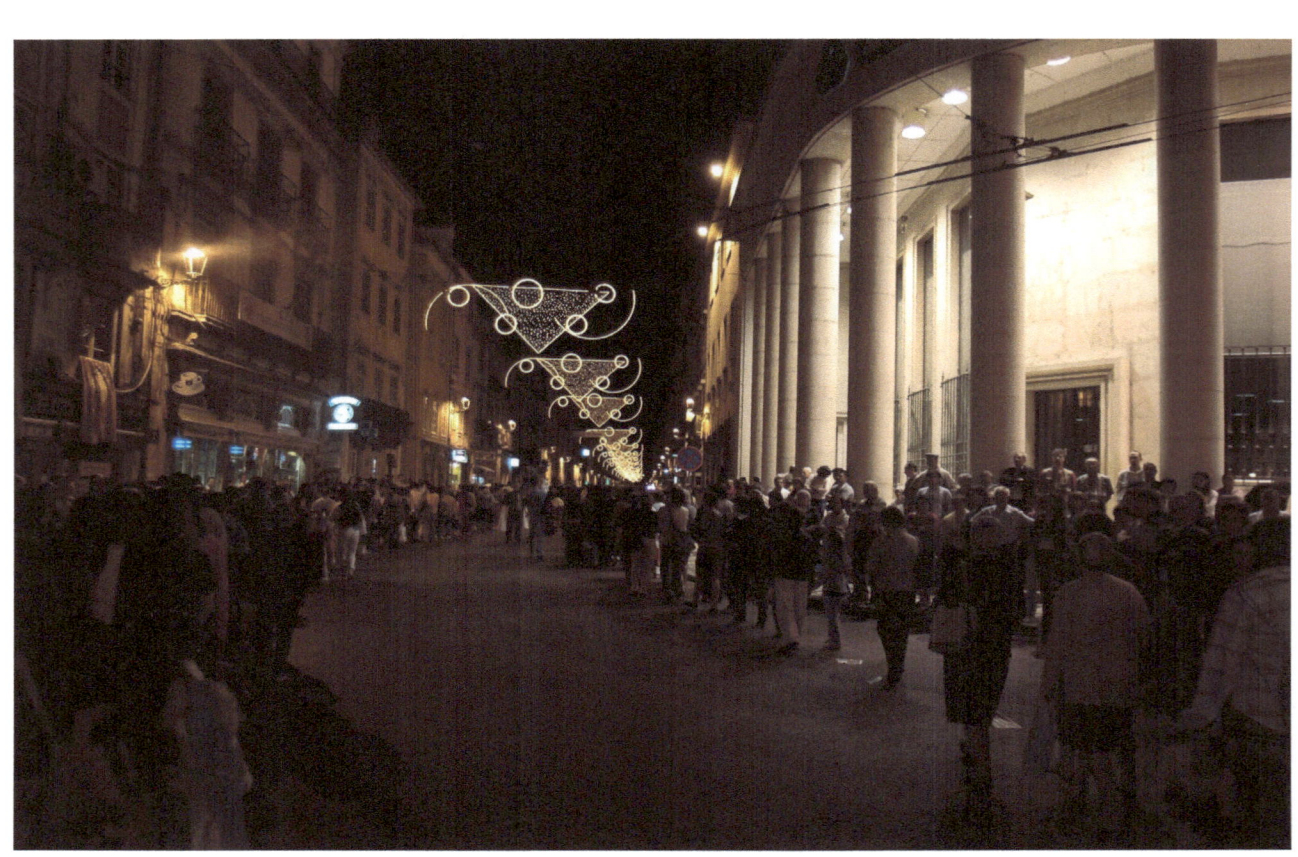

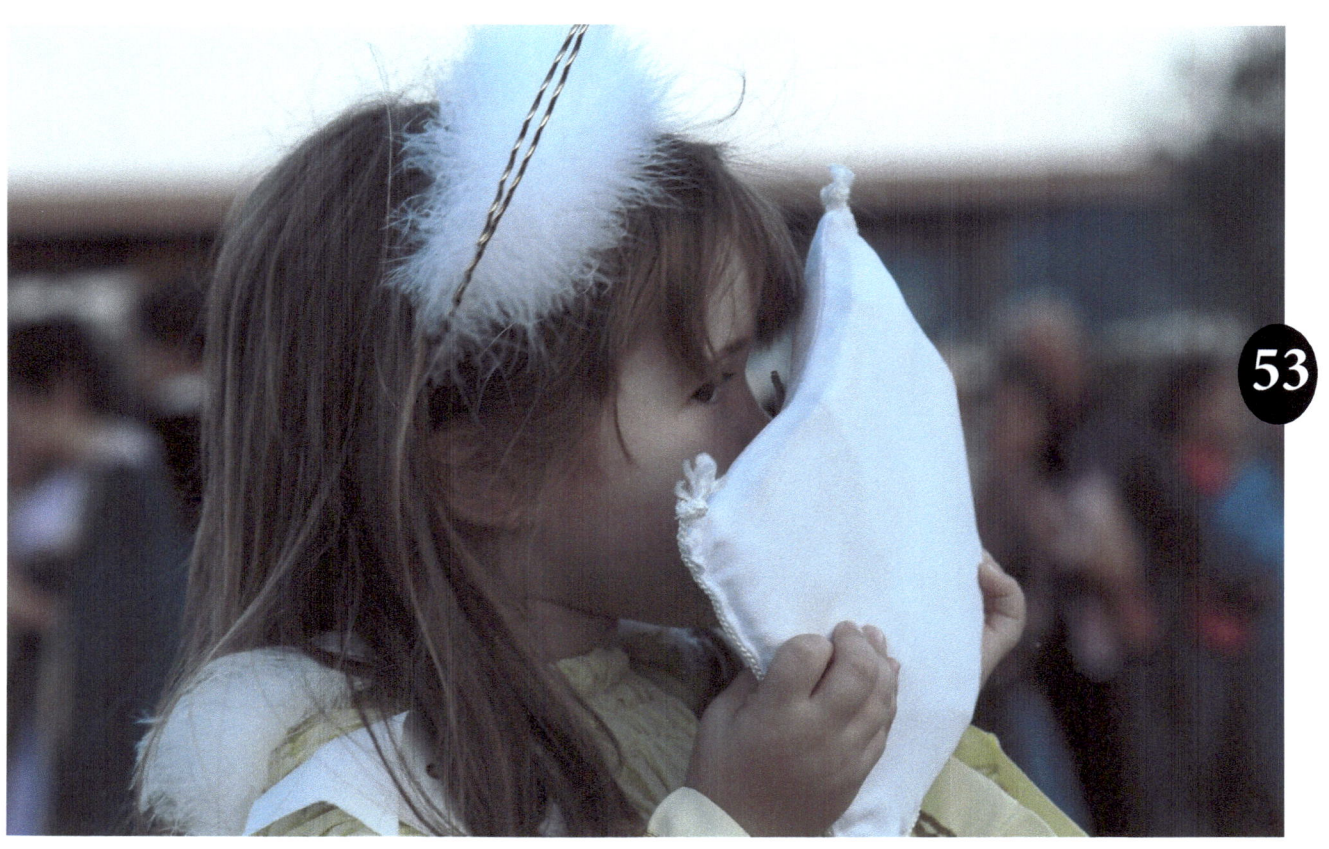

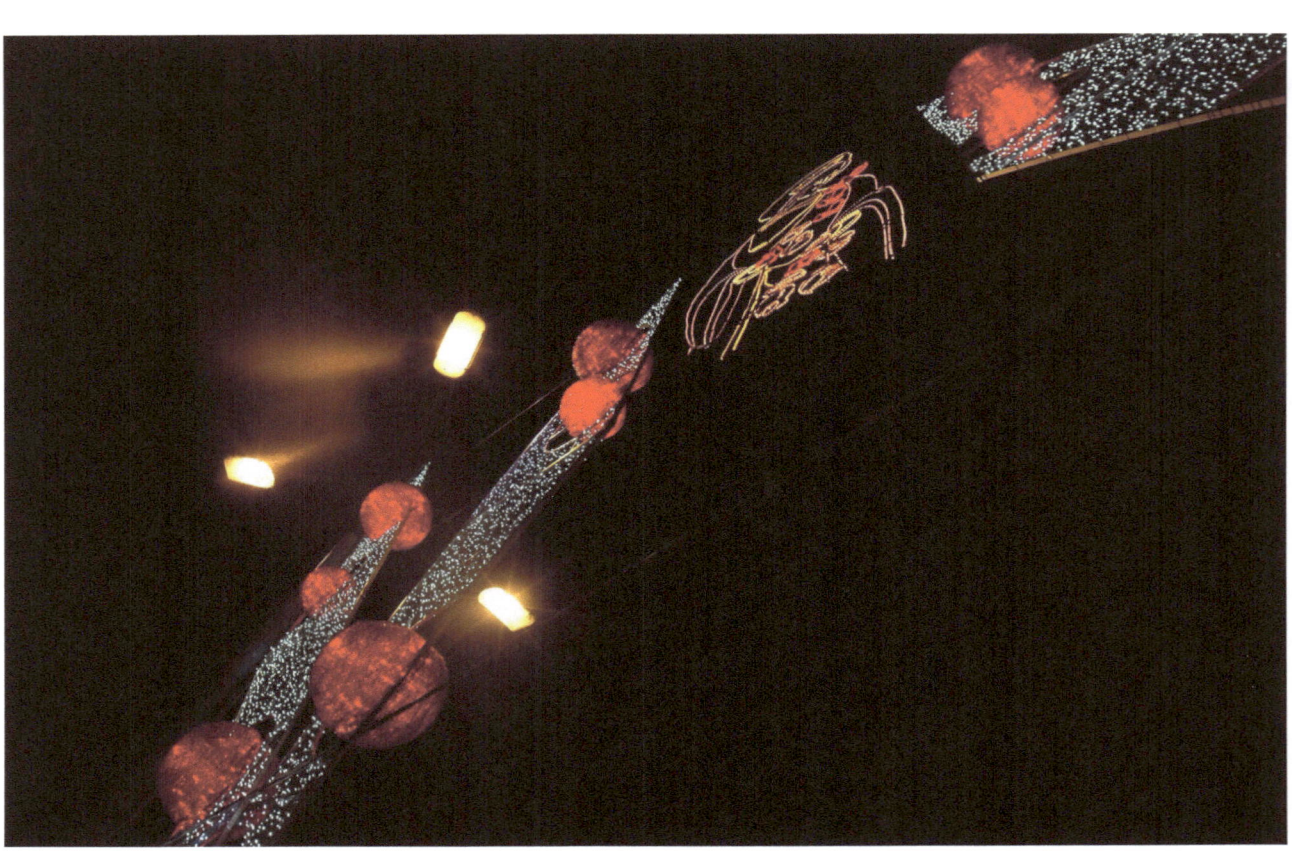

Also at amazon.com

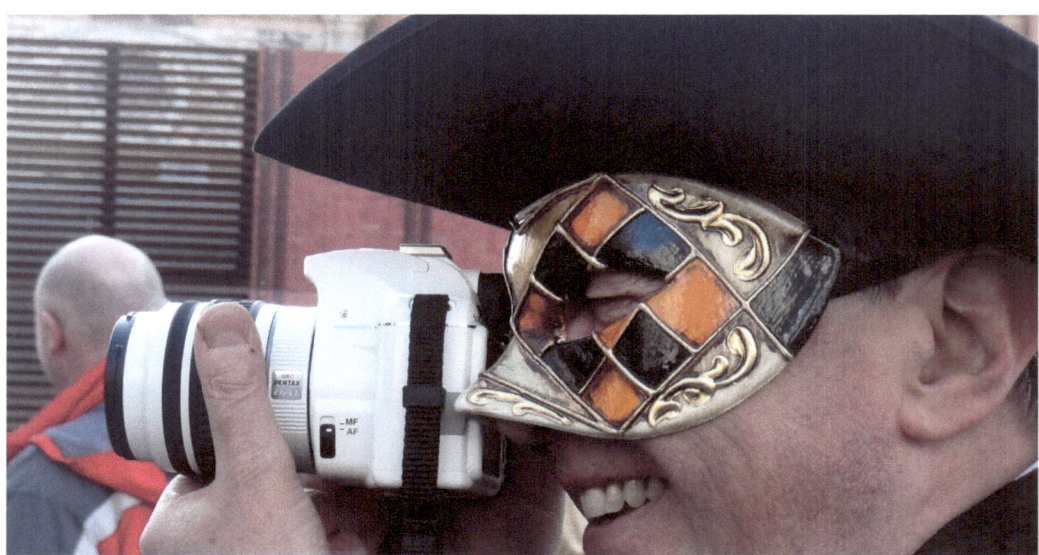